Window Dressings

Window Dressings

Beautiful Draperies & Curtains for the Home

Brian D. Coleman

Photographs by William Wright

GIBBS SMITH
TO ENRICH AND INSPIRE HUMANKIND

Paperback Edition
15 14 13 12 11   5 4 3 2 1

Published by
Gibbs Smith
P.O. Box 667
Layton, Utah 84041

www.gibbs-smith.com
Orders: (1-800) 748-5439

Designed by Linda Herman, Glyph Publishing Arts
Printed and bound in China
Gibbs Smith books are printed on either recycled, 100% post-consumer
waste, FSC-certified papers or on paper produced from sustainable PEFC-
certified forest/controlled wood source. Learn more at www.pefc.org.

Library of Congress Cataloging-in-Publication Data

Coleman, Brian D.
  Window dressings : beautiful draperies and curtains for the home / Brian
D. Coleman ; photographs by William Wright.—1st ed.
      p. cm.
  ISBN 978-1-58685-816-2 (hardcover)
  ISBN 978-1-4236-2339-7 (paperback)
  1. Windows in interior decoration—United States. 2. Draperies in
interior decoration—United States. I. Title.
  NK2121.C55 2006
  747'.3—dc22
  645.3   2005033874

Contents

Acknowledgments

The author and photographer would both like to thank the many designers and window workrooms around the country that helped make this book happen. Many people went out of their way to be helpful, but we would like to give special thanks to Lesley Petty, who introduced us to Margaret Davidson, our talented watercolor artist whose drawings gave the book an extra dimension and beauty. Bill would like to thank his wife, Pauline, and his parents, Will and Nancy for their support; and Brian would like to thank Howard for his patience with another book. Finally, both thank Madge Baird, an editor cum laude, for another job well done.

Introduction

Whether it's a window seat piled high with cushions in a cozy den, symmetrically placed french doors opening off a formal dining room, or just a single window in a small bedroom tucked under the eaves, windows are integral parts of every room's structure and design. In *Window Dressings* we explore beautiful examples across the country, from Nashville to New York, by visiting designers who have created successful window treatments in a variety of styles and approaches.

Divided into chapters based on the work of individual designers, *Window Dressings* offers ideas and inspiration for everyone. We have all been in beautiful rooms furnished in the best of taste, with fine furniture and accessories, except for the windows, which have been left bare. Sounds echo and are amplified in rooms without textiles, especially those without curtains. Draperies are what make the difference, absorbing sound, finishing the room and making it complete.

Window treatments help integrate the outdoors into the room. A well-designed drapery softens the edges of a window, framing the view and incorporating it into the room's overall design. Take, for example, a large breakfast-room bay overlooking a scenic lake in Michigan. A simple scalloped valance constructed in a pale green cotton check and accented with a colorful tasseled fringe covers the top of the large window, tying it into the room yet leaving the views intact. Or consider a sunny master bedroom overlooking a golf course in Richmond, Virginia. Bright floral cotton panels at the windows in pinks, blues and greens turn the room into a cheerful floral bower and help bring the vistas of the lush outdoor gardens and greenery inside.

Window treatments also set the tone for a room, whether it's formal and elegant, warm and welcoming or casual and comfortable. We travel to Chicago to visit an elegant town home on the Gold Coast, home of celebrity Marilyn Miglin. Its beautiful, formal interiors are accented by classic curtains of cream silk damask that hang beneath silk valances of festoons and cascades. The elegant formality is repeated in the dressing room, where swags of soft gray silk damask over the windows are reflected in the wall mirrors lining the long, opulent room.

Warmth and richness are the motifs of a large library in a substantial home on the New England coast. A coffered gold ceiling sparkles above the owner's collections of books and antiques. Cozy window seats are accented with burgundy-and-gold silk swags hung over rods punctuated by finials of rams' heads. The draperies' overall effect is at once rich and welcoming, inviting one to curl up with a good book and gaze over the crashing waves of the nearby Atlantic.

Country French informality was chosen as the theme for the windows of a starter home for a young couple in Rhode Island with their two small children. The small dining room was kept family friendly with custom painted bar stools for the children and whimsical balloon shades in a colorful cotton check that reflect the moods and interests of this growing family.

Color is another crucial function of good window design. Color sets the mood and atmosphere of a room, and nowhere is this more evident than at the windows. Well-known radio commentator Paul Harvey and his wife Angel's Chicago living room is awash in their favorite hot bubblegum pink with lively accents of turquoise and silver. The tall windows in the room are dressed using draw draperies with traditional cascades all in cheerful pink; accented with green and pink tassel trim, the draperies make the room seem like a warm and inviting sunset.

Or consider an active young daughter's room in Virginia. A pretty pale blue toile was chosen for a light and delicate look for both the walls and curtains. Centered on an antique wooden corona, the bed curtains are also constructed in the soft, summery fabric to create a serene and very feminine retreat.

Window color is also used to lend drama to a tiny pied-a-terre in New York's Greenwich Village. Its walls are glazed a deep burgundy and spectacular antique gold silk curtains that once belonged to Teddy Roosevelt, complete with their elaborate tassels and trims, are hung on the windows. The result is a richness and panache unexpected in such a tiny space.

Good curtains begin in the workroom, and professional advice is invaluable for anyone considering beautiful window treatments. We were fortunate to meet several very talented window covering professionals in the course of writing this book. Scot Robbins teaches classes in drapery construction and runs his own workroom in Nashville, where he produces expertly crafted draperies in a wide variety of styles and designs. Scot emphasizes the importance of "doing your homework first"; interview the workroom and look at examples of their work before you commit to a project, and make certain every detail has been documented and agreed upon and a signed contract obtained before you start. Scot recommends visiting the Window Coverings Association of America's Website (www.wcaa.org) for questions and referrals for workrooms in your area. Carlette Cormier, who runs her own workroom with her mother, produces exquisitely sewn draperies for the Savannah area and emphasizes the importance of the details, the custom touches that make the difference, such as micro cording, interlining and neatly covered cornice boards. Don't try to save money on an installer, she advises; hire a professional for the best results. Listen to your fabric, counsels Lesley Petty, who has made fine, custom-designed window treatments for the past fifteen years in Seattle. If a fabric is hard and stiff it may not want to be made into swags, and some weft-faced weaves spread horizontally and do not drape well. Interlining, Lesley muses, is much like cooking with cream instead of non-fat milk—you can adjust the fullness in the drapes using less yardage. And trims, she reminds us, do not have to be a perfect color match: a little contrast often helps accent the fabric and its design. An added bonus: exquisite hand-drawn watercolors by Margaret Davidson accompany the photographs, giving specific information on window treatment details that only a drawing can provide.

A comprehensive Glossary of Terms helps explain terms from *contrast lining* to *cornices* that are often confusing. And an extensive Resource Guide lists designers and window workrooms around the country, providing a helpful list of specialists in all aspects of window treatments and designs.

Window Dressings: Beautiful Draperies and Curtains for the Home is a must for anyone with windows, as a source of both inspiration and practical advice, no matter what style or period your home is. ◆

Adriana Scalamandre Bitter, the daughter of Franco Scalamandre, the famous silk textile and passementerie manufacturer, has grown up surrounded by fine textiles. Draperies were always an important part of her childhood and she recalls fond memories of the advent of spring, when her grandmother would remove the heavy, interlined winter curtains in the formal rooms of their home, hang them outdoors to be aired and dusted and replace them with lighter, unlined curtains for the summer months. While most people no longer make seasonal changes in their draperies, decorative textiles are still an important part of every well-designed interior. Adriana's love of fine fabrics is evident in her and husband Edwin's gracious Long Island home.

Legacy of Fine Fabrics
on Long Island

Adriana's legacy is shown in her country home on Long Island, where window treatments are carefully constructed with the finest fabrics and passementerie. The great room is the center of the newly built home with soaring thirty-foot ceilings and large windows facing private gardens. Meant for comfort and entertaining large family gatherings, the room was furnished with a mix of family heirlooms and favorite antiques, many inherited from Adriana's parents. The exquisite window treatments are shown to full advantage in this room, where panels of the Scalamandré silk "Simbolo Plaid" are lined with "Francesco" gold silk taffeta and finished with a soft, off-white-and-gold trim and "Louis XV Braid," a wide galloon. The plaid silk is swagged across the width of the window in soft folds and accented

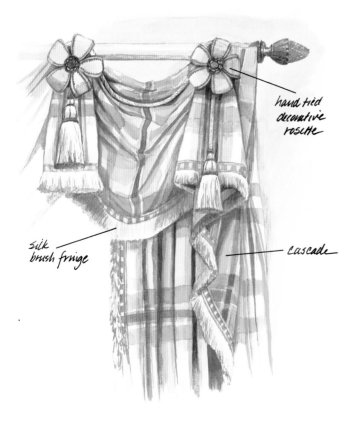

hand tied
decorative
rosette

silk
brush fringe

cascade

PREVIOUS OVERLEAF: *The great room is framed by magnificent window treatments in Scalamandré's cheerful silk "Simbolo Plaid" in peach, coral, green and gold. Panels fall simply to the floor and are finished with an off-white-and-gold trim and "Louis XV Braid" galloon. Jabots are lined with "Francesco," a gold silk taffeta, and accented with exquisite handmade rosettes covered in ivory silk and accented with "Radcliff" handmade silk tassels in ivory and rose. Adriana inherited most of the furniture from her parents, Franco and Flora Scalamandre, who purchased it on their trips abroad; the pine armoire was a surprise birthday gift from her husband, Edwin.*

OPPOSITE: *Each jabot is crowned with a handmade rosette, "Cornflower," and lined with "Francesco," a gold silk taffeta. The drapery pole is also covered in "Francesco." The walls were painted a custom maize yellow to complement the yellows and golds in the draperies.*

with jabots lined in the pale gold silk taffeta. The pièces de resistance are, of course, the magnificent handmade rosettes ("Cornflower") at the top of each jabot. Covered in ivory silk taffeta and bordered with a delicate, handmade trim, each is a work of art. A large handmade tassel in rose and gold ("Radcliff") hangs from a hand-wound silk cord as a finishing touch to each rosette. Attention to detail and the use of beautiful fabrics make this room's windows its crowning touch. ◆

Mark Scalamandre Bitter and his wife, Wiggie, both come from strong family traditions of good design. Mark's grandfather was Franco Scalamandre, founder of the textile company of the same name, and Mark is the company's third-generation co-president. Mark was raised with a knowledge and appreciation of fine textiles, from manufacture to installation. Wiggie was born in South Carolina and her family's history is one of gracious southern homes and interiors. Thus it is no surprise that their elegant home outside of New York City combines the best of both the North and the South for a sophisticated and stylish residence.

Sophistication and Style
in New York

When Mark and Wiggie Bitter first saw their current home outside New York City, they were attracted by its classically inspired interiors and well-thought-out design. Built in 1920, it required significant updating, including the addition of a new kitchen and family room. But once this was completed, the rooms' good proportions were a perfect fit for the couple, Mark providing the best of Scalamandré's soft furnishings and Wiggie adding her favorite family antiques.

Working with designer Jeff Lincoln, they upholstered the walls of the dining room with "Orleans," a textured silk damask in a warm red. Simple window treatments were constructed with colorful "Decatur Plaid," a silk taffeta in yellow, pink and white. Furnished with Wiggie's family antiques, such as an eighteenth-century Scottish huntboard between the windows and her blue-and-white

china collection, the room is both stylish and welcoming, just what a good hostess desires.

Both of Mark and Wiggie's girls have equally well-decorated bedrooms, giving them an excellent appreciation of good design as they grow up. The older daughter's room is centered on a beautifully designed bed with a canopy in "Cameo," a printed union cloth in coral and taupe on apple green. A decidedly feminine décor is evident in the cameos of classic maidens and floral motifs. The border of the headboard was shirred in colorful "Samba Stripe" cotton in coral, purple and green, and this was repeated on the bed skirt. The walls were papered in hand-printed, rose-colored "Compeigne" in a design of delicate flowers, with a floral border of "Ashley Swags" added above. Feminine and colorful, the room is perfect for their little princess. The younger daughter's room was planned to amuse and delight. With the assistance of interior designer Armando Guereca, the room was designed around "Kilkenny Cats," an amusing Edwardian toile of cats in human dress, strolling in the park on a Sunday afternoon. Used for papering the walls as well as the curtains, the blue-and-white toile was contrasted with cotton-and-silk "Bonnie Plaid" in sky and cream on the curtain cascades. A custom-designed shade in the same toile was added for privacy. What little girl would not be entertained in this room? ◆

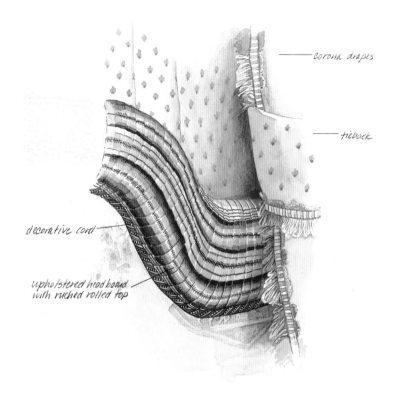

corona drapes

tieback

decorative cord

upholstered headboard
with ruched rolled top

PREVIOUS OVERLEAF: *Fit for a little princess, the older daughter's room has an elegant bed accented with a canopy in "Cameo," a printed union cloth in coral and taupe on apple green. Classical maidens and floral motifs are the fabric's themes. The walls are papered in delicate floral motifs of "Compeigne" in a soft rose hue. Notice the adjoining bath, which has curtains in "McGregor's Garden," a rose-on-cream, hand-printed toile based on a documentary early 1900s children's pattern of beguiling bunnies.*

OPPOSITE: *Cameos of classical maidens, floral swags and the delicate colors of blue, cream and rose make this an unabashedly feminine retreat.*

RIGHT: *The headboard border is shirred in "Samba Stripe" in pink and burgundy. An embroidered cotton was used for panels to line the back of the canopy and tiebacks. The panels are trimmed with cording and loop fringe in aqua and rose.*

OPPOSITE: *The youngest daughter's room is meant to amuse. It is designed around the blue-and-white toile "Kilkenny Cats," in curtains as well as wallpaper. A custom-designed roller shade was also made in the toile fabric for privacy. "Ribbon and Reed" was used as a wallpaper border.*

ABOVE: *Pleats with delicate bows and buttons accent the valance, which is trimmed with blue silk "Queen Street Galloon." Contrast is in sky and cream "Bonnie Plaid."*

RANDALL BEALE AND
CARL LANA

New York–based Randall Beale and Carl Lana have been designing together since 1992. From backgrounds as diverse as fashion and theater, they have been creating clean and elegant interiors with a refinement and creativity that sets them apart. While they have designed everything from corporate offices in Rockefeller Center to pre-war apartments, they were delighted when the owner of this mid-fifties home in West Palm Beach, Florida, asked them to help bring it into the twenty-first century while respecting its origins in mid-twentieth-century design.

Fabulous Fifties
in West Palm Beach

West Palm Beach is undergoing a housing renaissance as its older neighborhoods from the early and mid-twentieth century are being rediscovered by a new generation. This home, located in a historic neighborhood, was a typical split-level suburban ranch built in the mid-1950s. Beautifully sited on the intercoastal waterway, it had never been significantly altered and still boasted breathtaking views of Lake Worth and Palm Beach in the distance. An older couple who had lived in the home for many years sold it to the present owner with only one stipulation: that it would not be torn down. And while this was readily agreed upon, the new owner did undertake a major restoration, updating all of its systems with the latest technology. The interiors were lightened and the home was transformed into a casual and elegant pavilion with themes of coolness, simplicity and light.

The master bedroom, which looks onto the back-yard gardens and the infinity pool, was inspired by the best of the fabulous fifties. Hollywood and glamour were the period's buzz words; sexiness was in and nothing was considered taboo. Thus Carl and Randall selected shiny and sexy man-made fabrics for the room that would hold up to the Florida sun. "Wet" panels of a synthetic material from Glant Textiles, Italy, "Glant Patent Leather," were turned into gleaming white curtains topped by Rococo valances that were original to the house and re-covered in the same fabric. Roman shades constructed in "Giant Spa Cloth" in polyurethane and polyester, also from Glant Textiles, were added for nighttime privacy. Furnished with period furniture including a circa 1940 Lucite-and-lacquered console, and part of the owner's extensive art collection-from vintage pin-up photos of Bettie Page to glazed ceramic cats from France—the room has a "va va voom!" that is hard to resist. Midcentury modern has made a complete turn-about and come back home to West Palm Beach. ◆

PREVIOUS OVERLEAF: *The master bedroom was designed in a cool white palette with the best of the sexy and sophisticated fifties. Shiny, synthetic panels of "Glant Patent Leather" were used for the curtain panels and valances. Furniture includes a mix of period pieces, including Louis XVI–style fauteuils and a Lucite mirror-and-lacquered-wood console. Pin-up photos of Bettie Page, a sexy siren of the period, by Bunny Yaeger hang on the walls. The bench is upholstered in "Big Foot" white leather from Edelman Leather.*

RIGHT: *The shape of the window valances was taken from originals left in the house. The "wet" synthetic material used for the panels and valance was selected for its sexy yet simple look.*

OPPOSITE: *Windows are covered in wet synthetic panels of white "Glant Patent Leather" with valances in the same material. The Roman shades were made from another synthetic textile from Glant Textiles, "Giant Spa Cloth," which looks like latex and is "dry" appearing to contrast with the "wet" curtains. Part of the owner's art collection, including period pin-up photos and sculptures, add to the room's seductive appeal.*

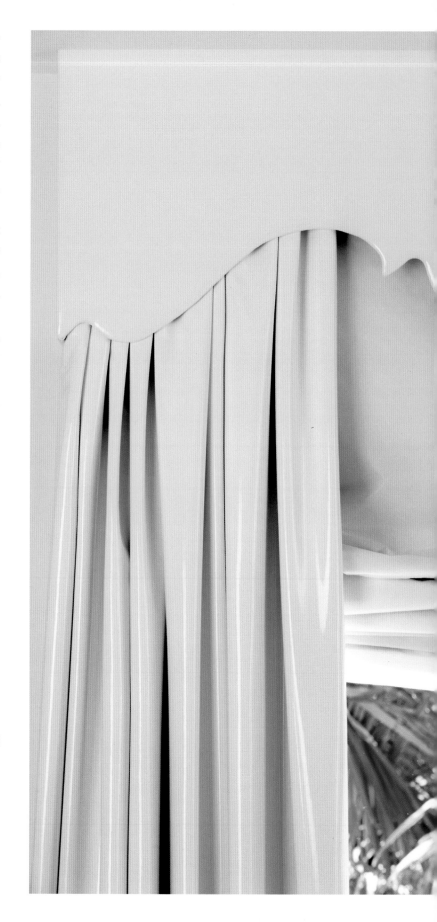

BENNETT WEINSTOCK

Bennett Weinstock didn't start out as a decorator; he obeyed his parents' wishes and became an attorney and an accountant instead. That is, until he turned thirty-nine, when he decided to "put away the shingle and pull out the chintz" and with his wife, Judie, opened his own interior design business. Specializing in English and Continental interiors, Bennett's attention to detail and use of color are his trademarks, and nowhere is this shown to better advantage than in his own home.

English Manor House
in the Sky

The Barclay has been one of Philadelphia's oldest and most prestigious hotels for many years. Built in 1929, it was designed originally as a luxury residential hotel in the most prestigious section of the city, Rittenhouse Square. But by the late 1990s, the building had fallen on hard times and was in danger of being demolished. Fortunately, a far-sighted developer stepped in and began restoring it to its former grandeur.

When Bennett heard of the project he was immediately enthralled. He and his wife, Judie, had spent their honeymoon at the Barclay and had many fond memories of the building. The grand rooms with ten-foot ceilings and large windows with views of Rittenhouse Square and downtown Philadelphia were still unchanged. And so they purchased two and a half of the former hotel suites

The office is upholstered in Old World Weavers' "Dieppe-Safram" in a rich terra-cotta red. The windows are covered in Christopher Hyland's colorful wool "Hyland" plaid. Anchored by a nineteenth-century "Sultanabad" Persian carpet and furnished with English antiques, the room has the feel of a British country house.

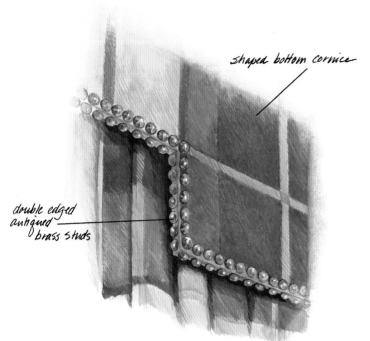

shaped bottom cornice

double edged
antiqued
brass studs

(5,500 square feet) and set about reconfiguring the space, replacing the entire interior to create a comfortable and stylish home in the sky, one inspired by the aesthetics of an English country manor.

Bennett designed an office for himself in a deep terra-cotta red by upholstering the walls with Old World Weavers' "Dieppe-Safram" linen-and-silk blend. Draperies were created from Christopher Hyland's masculine red-and-blue-plaid wool "Hyland" and a valance was constructed in the same fabric, the edges accented with double rows of antiqued brass tacks for a tailored look. Filled with antiques such as a metamorphic chair and collections of eighteenth-century stirrup cups, the room looks as if it were set in the English countryside.

The neighboring study was designed in complementary colors, as it adjoins the office. Walls were upholstered with Old World Weavers' rust-colored, cotton and silk, ribbed faille "Ritz." Jewel-toned draperies were constructed from Pierre Frey's "Mazarine," a multicolored silk, and skillfully accented with valance pleats in each individual color. Scalamandré's multicolored tassel fringe was added to the edges and a maize green contrast edging sewn to the

OPPOSITE, UPPER RIGHT: *Artfully constructed with each pleat in a different color, the valance is accented on top with a contrasting green silk moiré on the bias edge. The trim is a Scalamandré multicolored tassel fringe.*

OPPOSITE, LOWER LEFT: *Double rows of antiqued brass tacks accent the angularity of the plaids in the valance.*

ABOVE: *The study is upholstered in "Ritz," a ribbed faille from Old World Weavers in a warm terra-cotta. Colorful curtains in Pierre Frey's moiré silk "Mazarine" give the windows a festive look and complement the collections of eighteenth- and nineteenth-century English ceramics and paintings.*

valance top to provide finishing touches. The overall room is warm and inviting and glows with the blues, reds and greens of the upholstered walls and curtains.

Color was also emphasized in the living room, whose walls were painted a cheerful yellow with a soft milk paint. Fine English antiques, including an eighteenth-century George III armchair (1780) and a William and Mary (circa 1580) inlaid table were found to furnish the space. Curtains in Old World Weavers' "Grand Siecle," a watered, yellow silk taffeta with red-and-green floral accents, were chosen to coordinate with the sunny walls. Custom-made floral rosettes were commissioned from Scalamandré to accent the curtain tiebacks, and a custom-dyed ball fringe was hand made to match the reds and greens in the silk curtains.

Bennett prides himself on his wardrobe, and one of the most unusual and striking rooms in the home is his dressing room, whose built-in closets are upholstered in a mustard-colored French leather accented with antiqued brass studs. The walls are upholstered in Old World Weavers' "Topkapi Terre Cuite" in complementary earthen tones. Bennett found a pair of nineteenth-century hand-embroidered bell pulls on a trip to England and used those as valances. Curtains were sewn from Clarence House's ribbed silk "Rayure Selecte" in stripes of pink, blue, cream and green; wooden blinds were custom stained to match the woodwork. Bennett displays more of his extensive stirrup cup collection on a center table in his personal masculine retreat.

A rare American Aesthetic movement faux-bamboo bedroom set was found for the guest room, which was papered in Clarence House's terra-cotta-and-green toile "La Marchande D'Amount"; curtains were made in the matching fabric. A smocked valance with unpressed box pleats was designed to finish the window treatment. Woodwork, including the window blinds, was all painted a complementary terra-cotta for a coordinated and inviting look.

Bennett and Judie's master suite is upholstered in Clarence House's cotton "Damasco Cesari Gold" in creamy yellow-and-white stripes. Schumacher silk curtains in the pleasant floral plaid "Biella" were added with a soft valance of rolled pleats at the top. A green-checked taffeta was used as a bias trim at the top of the valance for just the right accent, and a hand-blocked floral double border by Zuber was added to the ceiling to complement the pattern in the drapes. Anchored by Stark's "Villandry" carpet in creams, reds and greens, the room is a romance of color and design. ◆

RIGHT: *An elaborate custom-made floral rosette from Scalamandré sets off the curtain tiebacks. Fringe was also hand made from Scalamandré and custom dyed in red and green to match the silk taffeta curtains.*

OPPOSITE: *The parlor is painted a sunny yellow and draperies are made from Old World Weavers' "Grand Siecle" in a watered yellow silk taffeta. Notice the valance, whose pleats are accented with a red silk rope cord twisted over their folds. Fine English antiques furnish the room.*

PREVIOUS OVERLEAF, LEFT: *Nineteenth-century needlepoint bell pulls were used to line the valances for a custom look.*

PREVIOUS OVERLEAF, RIGHT: *Bennett's dressing room has closets upholstered in soft French leather accented with antiqued brass studs. The walls are upholstered in a complementary mustard "Topkapi Terre Cuite" from Old World Weavers. Faille curtains from Clarence House, "Rayure Select," in pink, blue and green add color at the windows.*

OPPOSITE: *The inviting guest room is papered in Clarence House's terra-cotta red-and-green toile "Marchande D'Amount," and curtains are made in the matching fabric. A nineteenth-century Napoleon Quatre French opaline light fixture and a rare American Aesthetic faux-bamboo bedroom set give the room character and charm.*

ABOVE: *The guest room valance of Clarence House's "Marchande D' Amount" has unpressed box pleats smocked for added visual interest.*

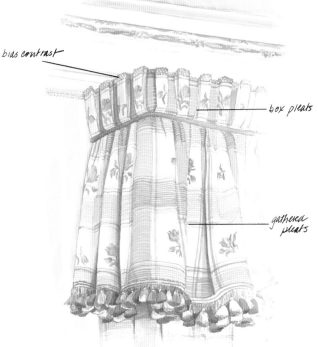

bias contrast

box pleats

gathered pleats

LEFT: *The master bedroom is beautifully coordinated in complementary creams, yellows, reds and greens. The walls are upholstered in Clarence House's "Damasco Cesari Gold" and the curtains are constructed from Schumacher's floral plaid "Biella" in yellow, red and green. An alcove for the bed was made to hide pipes that could not be moved.*

ABOVE: *The master bedroom curtains are accented with a rolled pleat valance set off by green-checked bias trim at the top. The floral motif is repeated in a hand-blocked Zuber wallpaper border on the ceiling.*

BRIAN COLEMAN

Writing a book on window treatments has been near and dear to my heart. One of my special interests is antique textiles, and I have created window treatments from a variety of vintage fabrics in every home in which I have lived. Some of my most spectacular drapes are in my pied-a-terre in New York's Greenwich Village.

Teddy Roosevelt
in Greenwich Village

When textile dealer friends told me about a pair of curtains that had recently come on the market, woven over a century ago for the 1893 Chicago World's Fair and having once belonged to Teddy Roosevelt, I was fascinated. With all of their original trimming intact, from the heavy gold fringe to the ornate cording and tiebacks—even the decorative brass moths used to anchor the cords—I was immediately smitten. Even though my apartment is tiny (350 square feet), I was able to use the historic curtains as a focal point, giving unexpected panache and elegance to what was originally a small New York tenement. The five-floor walk-up, originally built in the mid-1880s, was used to lodge up to a dozen people living and sleeping in the small rooms in shifts as they worked in factories and laborer jobs.

By the time I bought the apartment in the 1990s, it had been turned into a co-op and the small units had been updated with individual baths and kitchens. I wanted to preserve the original character of the apartment but make it a little more upscale than the original. (For an example of what a

PREVIOUS OVERLEAF: *The former tenement was redecorated with nineteenth-century furnishings including Hunzinger chairs upholstered in Scalamandré silk and British Arts and Crafts ceramics. The ornate gold silk curtains were made for the 1893 Chicago World's Fair and at one time belonged to Teddy Roosevelt.* OPPOSITE: *Green window shades were hand painted with a Christopher Dresser design of raining frogs. Vintage Victorian lace panels with hand-embroidered flowers and butterflies were* *found to drape beneath the curtains. Note the decorative wainscoting under the windows—it is actually Victorian linoleum recycled as a wall covering.* ABOVE: *Antique brass-and-opalescent-glass tiebacks were used for the cords holding back the curtain panels. Notice the Anglo-Japanese patterns woven into the silk and highlighted with metallic gold threads.*

tenement apartment really looked like, I highly recommend a visit to the Lower East Side Tenement Museum in New York.)

I had the walls glazed a warm, deep burgundy and began to gather an assortment of Victorian and Arts and Crafts furniture and ceramics. A decorative ceiling was hand painted in café au lait with gold, copper and turquoise accents from a design on a Minton tile.

The lush curtain panels were woven in golden brown silk, with intricate, Anglo-Japanese designs highlighted in gold metallic threads. They still had their original long, silk, chocolate-and-cream-colored fringe, intricately knotted cords and tiebacks and even a typically late-Victorian whimsical touch of decorative brass moths to hold the cords in the valance.

The fragile silk panels could be very easily ripped,

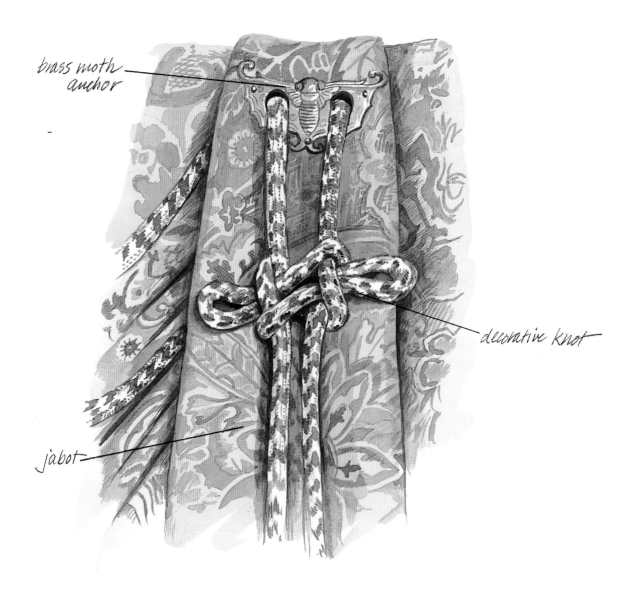

brass moth
anchor

decorative knot

jabot

so I had them backed with chocolate brown velvet to support their weight. Yazzolino Associates completed the remodeling of the draperies, including reconfiguring them to fit the space.

The ornate valances, with swags, long tails and thickly knotted cords and tiebacks were also very heavy, and so a cornice board was constructed and anchored into the wall with heavy metal braces beneath. I found antique off-white lace panels, hand embroidered with chenille butterflies and flowers, to hang behind the curtains. The windows were completed with schoolhouse-green window shades painted with a Christopher Dresser design of raining frogs for an appropriately Oriental touch. Ornate, opulent and definitely over the top, Teddy Roosevelt's curtains nonetheless give the former tenement panache. I like to think Teddy would approve. ◆

ABOVE: *The draperies are decorated with intricately knotted cream-and-chocolate silk cords and Oriental brass moths, all original to the curtains.*

Carlette Cormier has been in window design for nearly two decades. Her business, based in Savannah, is very much a family affair—her mother, Bug, helps with the sewing and her husband, Daryle, is her installer. Carlette both designs and fabricates window treatments and has won many awards for her work, including Workroom of the Year in 2004. Known for her skilled construction and attention to detail, it's no surprise that Carlette's workroom is one of the most popular in the area.

Marshland Magic
in Savannah

Working with Atlanta designer Patricia Reed, Carlette constructed elegant and colorful draperies for this graceful home outside of Savannah, Georgia. Built on a tranquil island, the home boasts lovely views of the surrounding marshlands and is decorated with traditional furniture and antiques the owners have collected. A clear, gem-like palette was selected for the dining room to tie together its richly hued fabrics and furnishings. Walls were glazed a rich terra-cotta and a lively silk taffeta plaid, Cowtan and Tout's "Pavilion Silk Check," was chosen to coordinate with the Oriental carpet's blues, reds, greens and golds.

Carlette explains that the window construction was a challenge with the taffeta's pattern of multiple horizontal bands of color. Fabric had to be cut for one side of the window, and then turned to create a mirror image for the opposite; silk is the only material with which this technique can be safely accomplished, she advises. Because the window is arched, a template was drawn first and then a frame was made for the valance, which was designed with swags and balanced with a central jabot. Fringed silk trim from Travers in matching rose, sage and gold was used to border both the valance and curtain panels. Needless to say, the homeowner was delighted when she saw her draperies, telephoning Carlette immediately with words of praise. ◆

OPPOSITE: *The dining room sparkles with the gem-like palette of reds, golds, greens and blues reflected in the silk taffeta curtains constructed in "Pavilion Silk Check" from Cowtan and Tout. Notice the coordinating horizontal bands of colors mirrored on opposite sides; this fine matching detail can only safely be accomplished with silk, Carlette advises. Dining room chairs are upholstered in a coordinating abstract arabesque linen, "Gourdes," from Old World Weavers, in ruby and cream. The crystal chandelier is an antique.*

ABOVE: *A cornice was built over the arched dining room window for the valance, which is swagged and dressed with a central jabot and tails on each side. Silk fringed trim in corresponding jewel tones of rose, gold and sage is an elegant finishing touch.*

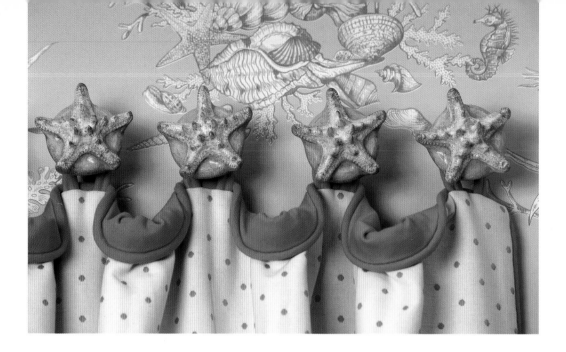

Low Country Color Outside Savannah

When the owners of this comfortable home on an island in the low country outside of Savannah consulted designer Nancy Sutton, they explained they wanted interiors that were bright and casual, rooms that reflected the surrounding water and wildlife outdoors. The guest bedroom was designed around a cheerful and amusing theme of sea life and the ocean. "Nautilus" wallpaper from Thibaut, featuring sea horses and shells in aqua and pink, was chosen, and Carlette constructed curtains in Stout Brothers' "Littleton," a pretty pink-and-white dotted swiss cotton. Purposefully left simple to avoid fighting with the bold wallpaper, the curtain panels were contrast corded on all four edges with Norbar's colorful cotton "Nanuet" in flamingo. Panels were kept flat, with loops made in the flamingo pink "Nanuet" and hung from hand-painted starfish medallions for a whimsical accent. The tops of the panels were then folded over from the back to show the bright pink contrast.

The cheerful pinks and blues were repeated on the bed with a dust ruffle in Duralee's pink cotton "Coral," and accent pillows were added in Thibault's "Nautilus" fabric that matches the wallpaper. This brightly colored guest room beckons with the best of low-country charm. ◆

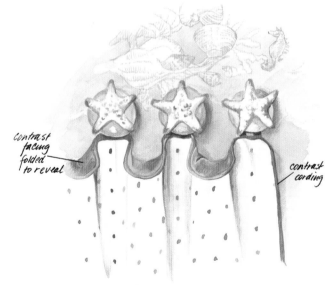

ABOVE, TOP: *Whimsical medallions of starfish were hand painted by local artist Paula Summerlin as amusing accents to the sea life theme. Contrast "Nanuet" fabric is a flamingo pink cotton.*

OPPOSITE: *The guest room is papered in Thibault's "Nautilus" in an aquatic theme of sea life and shells. The bright pinks and aquas are repeated in the bed coverings. Simple curtains are constructed from Stout Brother's "Littleton" in a pretty pink-and-white dotted swiss. Contrast cording in Norbar's cotton "Nanuet" in flamingo lines the borders of the panels as well as the turned-back tops of the panels.*

MARILYN WARNER
✎

Marilyn Warner has always loved beautiful fabrics and color, in particular the cheerful palate of French Country. After working with another designer she began her own business in 1997. Marilyn firmly believes homes should be comfortable and inviting and reflect the lives of the people who live in them.

Country French Elegance
in Richmond, Virginia

Marilyn's clients in Richmond, Virginia, share her love for colorful and elegant French Country design. So when they asked her to help them decorate their 1929 home, it was a perfect match. Designed by Duncan Lee, the stone-and-brick gabled home is named Fairway Ridge, as it is sited on a ridge overlooking the golf course of the Country Club of Virginia. Because the current owners have an active lifestyle with five busy children and a dog, they wanted interiors that were casual but still reflected their love of English and

French antiques. They began by gutting and expanding the kitchen, incorporating outdoor brick arches and a patio into its living area. Brunschwig and Fils' "Les Chanapans" in a sunny saffron was chosen for the kitchen draperies. The color was selected to coordinate with the kitchen cabinets, which had been hand-painted by Anne Thompson (a local specialty painter) in a pleasing antique mustard and green. The cotton curtains were backed with a bright red cotton check, also from Brunschwig and Fils, and a simple cut trim in a contrasting blue and white from Passementerie was used to tie both sides together.

The owners love deep colors, like the barn red they used in the adjoining dining room, which was furnished with an antique French gate-leg dining table and whimsical antiques such as a large, painted metal rooster. Ceiling-to-floor curtains in Cowtan and Tout's cotton "Hardwood Toile" in red and white were designed to lighten the room's palette, Their edges were trimmed with a Scalamandré wooden bell tassel and their backs are lined with Cowtan and Tout's cotton "Petersham Check" in coordinating red and white. Warm and cheerful, the room is now a favorite spot for dinner parties for the whole family.

The living room is the most formal room in the house. Woodwork, including custom built-in bookcases and a box beamed ceiling, was painted a deep, textured green for the look of an old English club. The green guided the choice of Cowtan and Tout's floral cotton

PREVIOUS OVERLEAF, LOWER LEFT: *An antique blue-and-white vase rests on the kitchen windowsill, whose curtains are backed with a contrasting red cotton check from Brunschwig and Fils and trimmed with a simple, blue-and-white cut fringe from Passementerie.*

PREVIOUS OVERLEAF: *Country antiques fill the kitchen and set the tone of a cheerful and whimsical room. Curtains from Brunschwig and Fils's "Les Chanapans" in a sunny yellow cotton were chosen to complement the French Country charm.*

ABOVE AND OPPOSITE: *More English and French antiques are displayed in the barn-red dining room, whose red-and-white toile curtain panels ("Hardwood Toile" from Cowtan and Tout) help lighten the room. The dining room draperies are trimmed with a Scalamandré wooden bell tassel fringe and their backs wear the lively contrasting cotton "Petersham Check" in red and white.*

"Coraux" for the windows, which were treated with a boxed valance and full-length panels. A colorful red-and-gold trim from Fonthill accents the cheerful colors of the draperies' floral design.

A light and pretty décor was chosen for the teenage daughter's room upstairs, which was furnished in pale blue and white. Centered on an antique corona, the bed curtains were made from Cowtan and Tout's soft blue cotton toile "Farnsworth"; the windows were also draped with the same fabric. A blue-and-white contrast cotton by Brunschwig and Fils, "Mignotte Stripe," was chosen for a subtle accent.

The master bedroom reflects the owners' love of pink and blue, with draperies and duvet constructed from Lee Jofa's cotton "English Floral." Scalamandré's tassel fringe in a matching blue was used to edge the curtain panels, which were backed with Brunschwig and Fils' "Island Stripe" cotton and finished with a contrasting rose cording from Schumacher, "Darien Check." As sunlight streams in, the pretty floral fabrics turn the room into a beautiful outdoor garden.

Marilyn reminds us that her talented curtain maker, Susan Schurtz from Tavern Hill Workroom (in Virginia), helped make all of the beautiful draperies possible. ◆

The living room is the most formal room in the house, its deep green woodwork enlivened with curtains in Cowtan and Tout's cotton floral "Coraux," in summery reds and greens, accented with red-and-gold Fonthill trim.

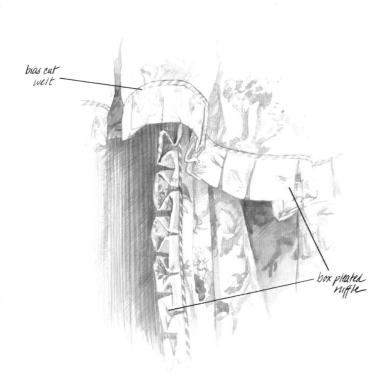

bias cut welt

box pleated ruffle

OPPOSITE AND ABOVE: *The teenage daughter's room was kept light and summery with Cowtan and Tout's light blue "Farnsworth" cotton toile, which was used on the windows, corona and bed pillows. Brunschwig and Fils' blue-and-white cotton* "Mignotte Stripe" *was used to contrast the toile; the edges of the curtains were accented with a handsome boxed pleat.*

LEFT: *The master bedroom is brought into bloom with Lee Jofa's pink, blue and green cotton "English Floral" used for the draperies as well as the duvet cover for the look of an English garden.*

ABOVE: *The master bedroom draperies are trimmed with Scalamandré's blue-and-white tassel fringe; their backs are accented with side hems in Brunschwig and Fils' blue-and-white cotton "Island Stripe." Note the subtle accent of rose cording (Schumacher's "Darien Check").*

DONNA MORRIS

Donna Morris never intended to be a decorator. But her home furnishings shop, French Twist, in East Greenwich, Rhode Island, was so popular that she bowed to her customers' demands and began designing interiors. Donna likes to mix and match styles and patterns to create a comfortable and inviting look that fits each person individually.

Starter Home Success
in Rhode Island

When Donna's clients asked her for help, they explained that although this was their starter home, they still wanted it to be special, personal and reflective of their lifestyle. A young couple with two toddlers, they wanted a child-friendly eating space off their kitchen that could also double as a formal dining room when they entertained. Donna chose a French Country theme with whitewashed Drexel Heritage chairs and table that coordinated with the kitchen cabinets. The chairs were upholstered in colorful plaid moiré and floral designs. Hand-painted bar stools were made for the children so they could sit either at the kitchen counter or at the table with the adults. Whimsical balloon shades were designed in Jane Churchill's "Bay Tree Check" and edged with box pleats in terra-cotta "Marwood Plain." A separate shade with points was added in green "Marwood Plain" and trimmed with Brunschwig and Fils's multicolored tassel fringe to complete the design. Family friendly yet formal enough for parties, the room was just what the young couple wanted. ◆

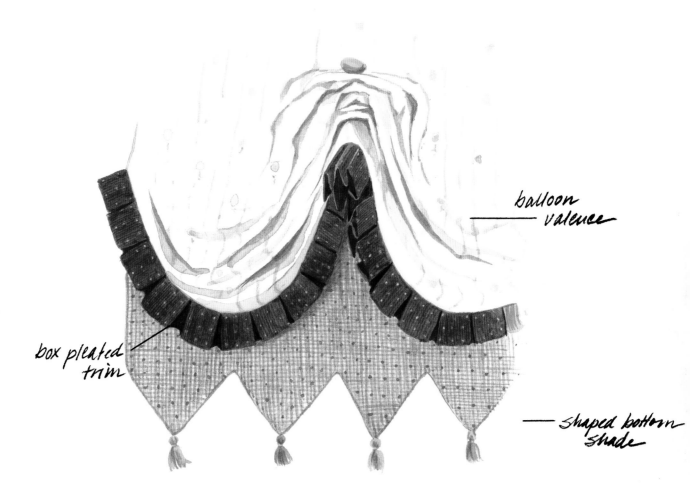

balloon
valence

box pleated
trim

shaped bottom
shade

PREVIOUS OVERLEAF: *The small eating space off the kitchen was turned into a family-friendly dining room with whitewashed French Country furniture from Drexel Heritage and a cheerful balloon shade over the window.*

OPPOSITE: *The colorful shade is constructed from Jane Churchill's cotton "Bay Tree Check" and accented with burgundy cotton box pleats in the coordinating terra-cotta "Marwood Plain." A scalloped shade in green "Marwood Plain" anchors the treatment with a whimsical note.*

FELICIA ZANNINO-BAKER

Felicia Zannino-Baker freely admits she is a passionate Italian who approaches her projects with an enthusiasm that is catching. A former model, her elegant personal style carries over to her work. Felicia designs interiors in a wide range of styles from contemporary to traditional, and strives to make each project a true reflection of the homeowners' own tastes and desires.

Old-World Charm
in Washington, D.C.

Felicia and her husband's historic home in Washington, D.C., reflects her design philosophy well. Built in 1929, the classically designed interiors have an old-world European look that Felicia carried through to the library. Paneled in dark-stained oak, the room is lined with bookshelves and centered on an ornately carved Renaissance Revival oak desk from the late

nineteenth century. Window treatments were kept simple with flat, Roman blinds made from a jewel-toned, 100 percent cotton textile "Mediaeval Alphabet," from Lee Jofa. The fabric was designed from illuminated manuscript letters in faded red, blue, green and gold, the tones echoing the colors of the leather book-bindings and accessories in the room. Now a favorite retreat for the entire family, the library reflects the family's love of literature and classic design. ◆

ABOVE: *Lee Jofa's multicolored cotton "Mediaeval Alphabet" was used for the library's Roman blinds.*

RIGHT: *The library is lined with dark-stained oak bookcases for an old-world elegance. Roman blinds were chosen for the windows in Lee Jofa's "Mediaeval Alphabet" cotton to complement the classic look. Furnished with family memorabilia and antiques such as the ca. 1900 French chandelier, the room is a favorite retreat.*

Contemporary Update
in Baltimore

Built in 1977, this suburban Baltimore ranch home is beautifully nestled in a wooded glen. Floor-to-ceiling glass walls and clean lines make the home still attractive and inviting a quarter of a century later; but when its current owners purchased it three years ago, it needed a contemporary update. Most rooms required only cosmetic changes, while the kitchen required a complete makeover. Felicia had its orange, brown and white laminate cabinets replaced with elegant oak cabinetry and granite countertops. "Primavera," an Indian cotton-and-viscose woven-and-embroidered textile from Donghia-Pollack was selected for the Roman shade window treatment, with its texture being as important as its color and design. Felicia chose earth tones of taupe, sage, eggplant and camel to expand the feeling of nature found throughout the house.

Earthy tones in multiple textures repeated in the master bedroom again emphasize the relationship of the house to its sylvan setting. The wall behind the bed was upholstered in Scalamandré's taupe "Etrecy," a textured jacquard inspired by French design. The headboard was upholstered in "Lunaria," an elegant mocha-colored silk from Pindler and Pindler that features a stylized, meandering floral vine. The sheer side curtains of the canopy bed are done in "Bouvier," from Pindler and Pindler, in a soft bamboo color. The curtains, along with raw silk-and-chenille pillows, combine natural textures, patterns and colors to give a feeling of a serene and secluded woodlands escape. ◆

ABOVE: *"Primavera," which means "spring" in Italian, is used for the kitchen's Roman blinds. Multi-textured and multi-toned, the fabric coordinates with the colors and textures of the rest of the interior, which reflects the home's surrounding woodlands.*

OPPOSITE: *The remodeled kitchen's Roman shades are fabricated from an embroidered cotton-and-viscose blend from Donghia-Pollack. The warm earth tones of the fabric are reflected in the creamy granite countertops and soft wood tones of the cabinetry.*

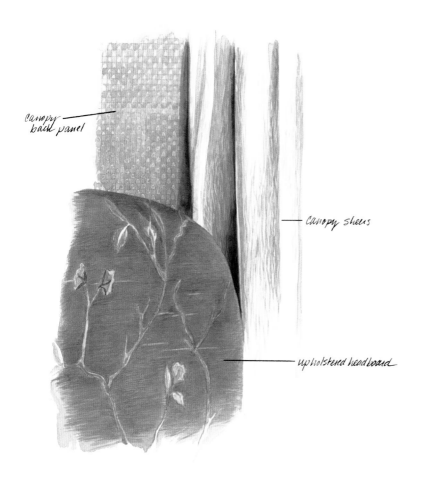

canopy
back panel

canopy sheers

upholstered headboard

RIGHT: *Earth tones and textures make the master bedroom serene and inviting. Walls are custom finished in a striped taupe glaze, and the bed canopy is constructed with soft, bamboo-colored side sheers of "Bouvier," a 100 percent polyester from Pindler and Pindler. Scalamandré's "Etrecy," a textured jacquard, covers the wall behind the headboard, while Pindler and Pindler's mocha silk "Lunaria" is on the headboard and is repeated on the dust skirt. "Tranquil Sateen" in warm stone, from Donghia-Henry Calvin, makes the perfect comforter and is repeated on the underside of the canopy.*

John Rolland has been an interior designer based in Philadelphia for more than fifteen years, specializing in sophisticated English- and French-inspired interiors. His own apartment in the Barclay, one of Philadelphia's classic prewar buildings on Rittenhouse Square, is a testament to his skills of combining fine continental antiques with the best of classic fabrics and furnishings. When he bought the apartment several years ago, it required total restoration. John transformed the suite of spacious rooms with views of Rittenhouse Square into a timeless and elegant home.

Classic Continental Elegance
in Philadelphia

John Fowler, one of England's best-known decorators, has always been a source of inspiration to John Rolland, who designed his master bedroom as an ode to the famous designer. The walls were upholstered in Brunschwig and Fils's silk "Woodbury Moire" in soft beige and gold, and a handsome, hand-painted English satinwood, canopied bed from Julia Gray was chosen. An Adams-style satin wood linen press, also from Julia Gray, handles storage, including the television. Curtains were selected in Clarence House's floral chintz "Lettres de Mon Jardin" in soft blues and beiges, and the same fabric was used for the bed canopy and headboard. The swags and jabots of the window valances were lined with Rose Cumming's "Ribbons," a lively blue-and-white cotton chintz. "Ribbons" was repeated on a comfortable armchair and ottoman, as well as in the shirred curtains at the head of the bed. London shades, softly shirred pulls in Brunschwig and Fils's "Bijou Sheer Natural," were added at the windows to

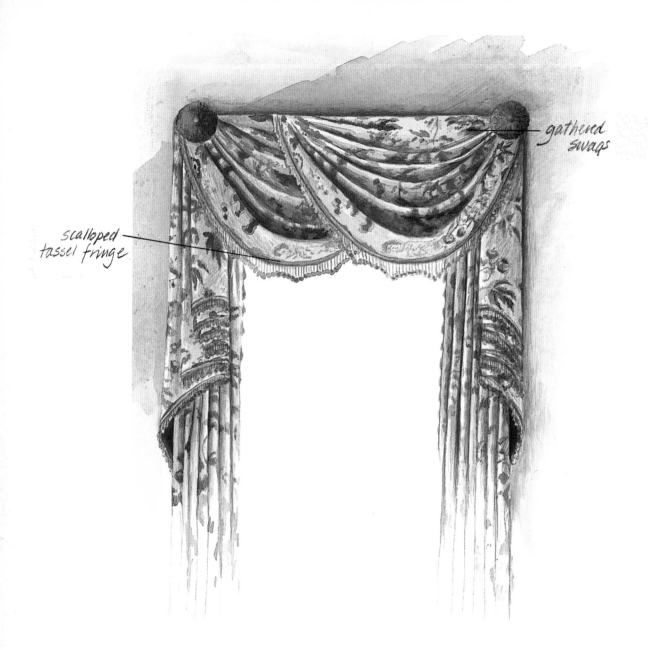

gathered swaps

scalloped tassel fringe

soften the afternoon sun. Furnished with John's collection of antique blue-and-white Oriental ceramics, the room has a timeless and classically English appeal.

The large parlor is the heart of the apartment, its central, broad window overlooking the gardens of Rittenhouse Square. The walls were upholstered in Scalamandré's gold, tone-off-tone cotton damask "Diana" and trimmed with a gold silk gimp. Brunschwig and Fils' "Villiers," a warp-print silk taffeta in multi-colored floral designs on a cream ground, was used for the window draperies and valance, with tails lined in Brunschwig and Fils's yellow "Alma Taffeta Stripe" for an elegant contrast. Clarence House's multicolored silk tassel fringe "Meches" was used to border the valance and drapery panels, and opulent silk tassels and rosettes add elegant accents. London sheers were again used to diffuse the sunlight.

The pillow reads: I'm making my favorite thing for dinner...Reservations

PREVIOUS OVERLEAF: *The master bedroom is designed with the theme of traditional English comfort. A hand-painted Adams-style English satinwood bed from Julia Gray centers the room. Curtains are constructed from Clarence House's "Lettres de Mon Jardin" in floral, blue-and-beige chintz and lined with Rose Cumming's chintz "Ribbons" in a coordinating blue-and-white pattern. The bed linens are "Pratesi" from Italy. Antiques, including an English George III marquetry table between the windows and blue-and-white Chinese ceramics, add to the timeless appeal.*

ABOVE: *The bed curtains are made from Rose Cumming's blue-and-white chintz "Ribbons," while the headboard is shirred in Clarence House's "Lettres de Mon Jardin." Bed pillows were hand painted in the same floral chintz design to add to the tailored look. Bed linens are from Italy.*

An impressive red-lacquered George III secretary, circa 1780, anchors the end of the parlor and holds some of John's extensive Rose Medallion collection. A comfortable lounge chair was upholstered in a gold Louis XV–style jacquard and combined with English Regency furnishings, including a tilt-top breakfast table and four dining chairs; the breakfast table in front of the window has now become a favorite spot for dining and watching the activities in the Square below. An Aubusson rug by Mark Phillips, Ltd., pulls the room together and adds to the classic continental look. ◆

ABOVE: *The curtain panels are composed of four layers of fabric to drape and hang well (from left to right): Clarence House chintz trimmed with a taupe fringe from Colefax and Fowler; cream flannel lining; matte black unglazed chintz for sun block (soft rather than the traditional stiff black-out material); white sateen inner lining.*

OPPOSITE: *Hand-painted floral chintz pillows rest on an armchair upholstered in Rose Cumming's "Ribbons" in a beautifully coordinated mélange of color and pattern.*

LEFT: The elegant parlor is centered on a large window overlooking Rittenhouse Square. Curtains in Brunschwig and Fils's "Villiers," a floral silk warp print, are finished with an elegantly swagged valance lined with "Alma Taffeta Stripe" in coordinating yellow stripes. The walls are upholstered in gold silk "Diana" from Scalamandré. Furnishings are a mixture of English Regency and Chippendale antiques. The valance is accented with Clarence House's multicolored "Meches" silk tassel trim and hand-made silk rosettes. London shades of Brunschwig and Fils's "Bijou Sheer Natural" are hung against the window to help screen the afternoon sun.

ABOVE: Contrast lining in Brunschwig and Fils's "Alma Taffeta Stripe" is a subtle accent in the tails of the valance and highlights the multicolored silk tassel trim and tassels from Clarence House.

KENT KIESEY

Kent Kiesey started his career as an interior designer with Marshall Field and Company in Chicago, and founded his own firm in 1992. Kent likes to design rooms with classical beauty and comfort; his interiors have a look of understated elegance that is much appreciated by his clients.

Serenity in the Woodlands
of Michigan

When the owners of a busy dental practice decided to retire, the serenity of the Michigan countryside was just what the doctor ordered for a slower, more enjoyable lifestyle. And so they built their dream home on twenty wooded acres above a scenic, slow-flowing river. Large windows were designed across the back of the home to take advantage of the verdant views.

The owners consulted Kent to help furnish its interiors in an elegant and comfortable style, something with color and flair that wouldn't obscure the vistas they enjoyed from nearly every window. The breakfast room, set in a bay off the kitchen, was given the look of a tropical green conservatory. Kent chose the straightforward Scalamandré green cotton "Dally Check" for a simple valance over the top of the bay, its outline following the angles of the window. Accented with scalloped edges laid upon a flat lambrequin, the valance was finished with a multicolored Houlès cotton trim and provides the perfect accent for the large window without obscuring the sweeping

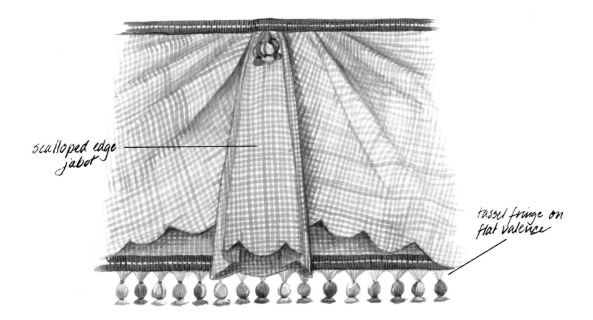

scalloped edge jabot

tassel fringe on flat valence

lawns and river beyond. Color was added with McQuire chairs covered in a busy tropical linen print, "Galvaro," from Old World Weavers and a hand-blown, multicolored glass-and-iron Italian chandelier for a dash of sparkle above.

The dining room overlooks a wildlife garden set against a redbrick wall and its floor-to-ceiling curtains were kept simple to help frame the view through the french doors. The walls of the room were upholstered in a honey-colored cotton damask from Christopher Norman, "Monteverdi," and trimmed with Samuel and Sons' wine- and-gold "Venus" gimp. Simple curtain panels with continental pleats were constructed from Scalamandré's multicolored woven "Perrault," from their Colony Collection, and accented with Cowtan and Tout's gold, green and wine "Colette" trim for an elegant and understated look. Colefax and Fowler's "Brisbee" sheers were set as partial door coverings beneath the drapes. Favorite antiques, including a French crystal chandelier and grandfather clock, make this a formal but still personal room.

The library, paneled in handcarved oak, looks like it has been there for generations but in reality is completely new. When first installed, the paneling was very dark and the room appeared much too somber. So Kent had the walls lightened by first distressing them with chains, hammers and screwdrivers; whitewashing them; with the final marks being faux fly specs, created by splattering black paint off a stiff toothbrush. Scalamandré's "Adam Plaid" silk taffeta in a golden tangelo was chosen for the windows. The panels were left unlined so that late-afternoon sunlight could flood the room, making it glow like a beautiful sunset. The draperies were hung from a simple brass rod and held in place by silk cord-and-tassel tiebacks from Houlès; the geometric pattern of the dignified silk fabric contrasts handsomely with the sinuous curves in the oak wall paneling. ◆

PREVIOUS OVERLEAF: *Sweeping views of the lawns and river were kept intact in the breakfast bay with a simple, shallow valance with scalloped edges over a flat lambrequin, all in Scalamandré's cheerful green "Dally Check."*

OPPOSITE: *A colorful, Italian hand-blown-glass-and-wrought-iron chandelier picks up the colors in the valance, including the multicolored cotton tassel trim from Houlès.*

LEFT: *In the dining room, multicolored woven panels from Scalamandré ("Perrault" from their Colony Collection) were hung in continental pleats from a brass rod over the french doors. The walls were upholstered in a honey-colored cotton damask ("Monteverdi") from Christopher Norman for a lighter but still sophisticated look.*

ABOVE: *Cowtan and Tout's "Colette" trim in gold, wine and green was used to edge the curtain panels, their floral motifs echoing a wildlife garden outside the windows.*

ABOVE: *Unlined, loose-fitting silk taffeta panels were chosen for the library windows in Scalamandré's golden tangelo "Adam Plaid," to let the sunlight stream in and the room glow with the warm color of the end of the day. Rusty, the family chow/collie mix, enjoys the room as much as his owners.*

OPPOSITE: *Late-afternoon sun lights up the silk taffeta panels of "Adam Plaid," loosely tied back with Houlès' silk-and-cord tiebacks. The oak panels are new, distressed and whitewashed to give them age and patina. Fabric panels of Old World Weavers' "Style Oriente" were inset in the paneling to add warmth and intimacy.*

A Passion for Pink
in Chicago

When Kent Kiesey first met the well-known radio commentator Paul Harvey and his wife, Angel, more than twenty years ago, they gave him a test: find a lamp for their hall table. Kent found an antique opaline table lamp that was a perfect fit, and a relationship was begun that has lasted for more than two decades. Kent understands the Harveys' aesthetic, particularly their love of strong color, and helped them design their parlor around their favorite shade—bubblegum pink.

A formal direction was chosen for the draperies to reflect the character of the home, a two-story Georgian stone house with a traditional center hall with a black-and-white checkerboard tile floor. Draw draperies in Manual Canovas cotton duck fabric were designed for the large formal parlor, and the valances were dressed up with festoons and cascades—all, of course, in bubblegum pink. Custom-colored Merwitz Textiles cotton tassel trim in pink and green was used to line their edges. Walls were painted the same cheerful pink, and comfortable, matching tufted loveseats were covered in a textured Brunschwig and Fils rose floral cotton chintz. Subtle accents of turquoise and silver make the room come alive in a glow of sunset colors, and it is one of the Harveys' favorite spots both night and day. Pink was continued upstairs in the master bedroom, with draperies constructed in a symphony of pink and turquoise. A Scalamandré pink moiré silk was used, and the valance's necktie pleats were highlighted on top with round glass balls. Custom-designed turquoise-and-pink trim by Merwitz Textiles of Chicago was a delicate final flourish. The pink is both psychologically soothing and enveloping, the Harveys explain, and makes the rooms feel welcoming, as if they were wrapping their arms around you as you step inside. ◆

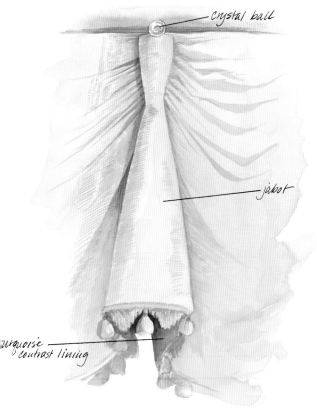

crystal ball

jabot

turquoise contrast lining

PREVIOUS OVERLEAF: *Paul and Angel Harvey's bubblegum pink parlor is at once formal and comforting, all in soothing shades of pink. The draperies are constructed with valances of festoons and cascades, accented with custom Merwitz pink-and-green cotton tassel fringe.*

OPPOSITE: *The master bedroom is bubblegum pink as well, with draperies fabricated from a Scalamandré pink moiré silk and the valance highlighted at the top with reflective glass balls for an opulent touch.*

TOP LEFT: *Turquoise-and-pink trim was custom designed from Merwitz Textiles to delicately accent the bedroom draperies.*

ABOVE: *A doorway adjoining the music room is also draped with matching panels and a valance in a bright pink Manual Canovas cotton to emphasize the symmetry and balance of the room.*

A Passion for Pink 89

Gold Coast Elegance

Marilyn Miglin, Chicago beauty authority, author and television personality is much loved and admired for her elegant style, wit and charm, as well as her dedication to community (April 15th is Marilyn Miglin Day in Chicago, in honor of her philanthropic work). Marilyn's townhome, located on Chicago's Gold Coast, is in an area of graceful nineteenth-century mansions bordering Lake Michigan. Built in 1871 after the Chicago Fire, it was constructed of brick and stone like most homes of the period, and Marilyn has worked with Kent over the years as she has slowly restored it.

The dressing room is the most dramatic space in the home—a long, narrow room adjoining the master bedroom. Wall mirrors cover the entire room and conceal closet doors, helping expand the

LEFT: *Marilyn Miglin's dressing room is stylish and dramatic. Closet doors are covered with mirrors to help expand the narrow space. An elaborate valance with cascades and festoons in a Scalamandré gray silk damask covers the window across the back and is reflected in the mirrors, giving the room a deeper and even more luxurious look.*

ABOVE: *The gray silk damask cascades in the dressing room are trimmed with silk tassel trim of the same color. A sheer, silk pull-up shade was designed to provide privacy but still allow the afternoon sun to light the room.*

space visually. The room is centered on a large floor-to-ceiling window that overlooks the back garden and receives the afternoon sun, and so Kent designed a woven, sheer silk thread pull-up shade to diffuse the light. A classic and elegant valance was built across the top of the window, with festoons and cascades in a soft gray Scalamandré silk with accents of silk tassel trim in the matching color. Striking and sexy, the dressing room aptly reflects Marilyn's stylish personality.

The main floor of the home was never significantly altered, and the adjoining living and dining rooms have been decorated in a coordinated palette of classic creams and golds. Kent designed lush draperies for the large window in the living room in a Scalamandré silk the color of a "baking powder biscuit," a subtle and sophisticated hue that coordinates well with the antique gold tones of the furniture and lighting. A valance of elaborate cascades and festoons highlighted with crossed bowties at the top and a gathered valance underneath was added, and silk tassel trim in a matching cream was placed on the leading edges of the draperies and festoons for a more lavish and finished look. Classic matchstick shades with mirrored inserts in the Roman Fold style, custom colored in the same biscuit cream, were added underneath the drapes for privacy. Similar draperies were installed in the dining room, where mirrors along one wall lend drama and depth to the space. Tailored and elegant, the rooms have a classic look that never goes out of fashion. ◆

PREVIOUS OVERLEAF: *Elaborate draperies of biscuit-colored silk damask by Scalamandré were designed for the living room. The intricate valance features festoons and cascades highlighted with crossed bowties at the top and a swagged valance underneath; the fabric was lined and interlined to give it more body and to drape well.*

ABOVE: *Thick cream silk tassel trim from Scalamandré lines the dining room valance, giving it more richness and body. The walls are papered in a custom paper from Winfield Design of overlapping Japanese fans.*

OPPOSITE: *The adjoining dining room has draperies and valance matching the living room's design, seen here reflected in the large, beveled-glass wall mirror.*

Gorgeous Garret
in Chicago

Not all garrets are gloomy. Take, for example, the top-floor bedroom in a Chicago home that Kent has transformed into a stylish and welcoming guest retreat. Built in 1880, the stone house has been methodically restored by the owners, two physicians who love all things Oriental.

Sloped ceilings were left intact on the third floor, where a bedroom and bath were created for guests. Kent had the bedroom walls upholstered in Scalamandré's red-and-white "Pillement Toile," and

ABOVE: *A flat valance reminiscent of a Japanese pagoda was constructed for the windows to continue to Oriental theme. Guilded wood bells provide an extra flourish.*

RIGHT: *The third-floor bedroom was transformed into a cozy guest retreat with Scalamandré's red-and-white "Pillement Toile" used on the walls and curtains. The sofa was slipcovered in the same fabric as well. The gold-and-chocolate ocelot-patterned carpet provides an appropriate counterpoint to the toile. The bed is an antique, ca. 1860, with nickel-plated headboards and footboards.*

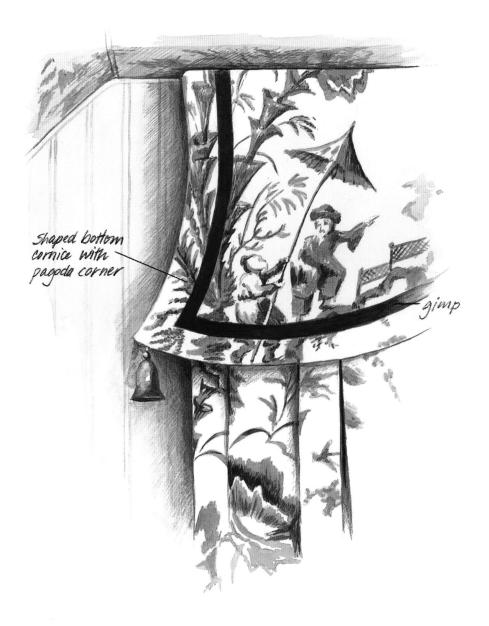

Shaped bottom cornice with pagoda corner

gimp

continued the theme throughout the room, constructing simple curtains on the windows, slipcovers for the furniture and pillows on the bed in the cheerful cotton pattern for a warm and intimate look. Kent designed a flat valance for the window in the shape of a pagoda, complete with gilded wooden bells whose lines echo the slope of the ceiling. Every space was used: a small corner under the eaves was draped with more toile and made into a cozy corner with the addition of a small reading chair, actually a theater seat upholstered in a coordinating red-and-white Scalamandré cotton plaid. The adjoining bathroom was finished in a complementary theme, papered with Colefax and Fowler's "Selwood Stripe" in red and cream. A shower curtain and Austrian puff valance were added in "Salwin," a Christopher Norman fabric similar to "Pillement Toile."◆

LEFT: *The guest bathroom continues the red-and-white theme with striped wall and ceiling paper from Colefax and Fowler, "Selwood Stripe," for a tented look. Christopher Norman's "Salwin," similar to "Pillement Toile," was used for the Austrian puff valance and shower curtain; Scalamandré's "Gold Jade" trim finishes the bottom of the valance.*

BELOW: *A cozy corner was created by curtaining off a corner for reading with more "Pillement Toile." The chair is actually a theater seat with tufted arms that are semi-slipcovered with superimposed festoons on the sides and kick pleats at the corners in a red-and-white cotton plaid from Scalamandré.*

RICHARD LOOMIS AND DAVID HERCHIK

Richard Loomis and David Herchik have run their Washington, D.C.–based design firm, JDS Design, for more than two decades. They have no distinct style they like to emphasize but, rather, try to reflect the client's individual taste in each project. With their own drapery and upholstery workshop and an extraordinary eye for antiques and unusual furnishings, they have created many unique custom interiors.

Italian Villa
in Washington, D.C.

The owners of this large home in a Washington, D.C., suburb had built their home in a traditional Williamsburg style but weren't satisfied with the results. Both husband and wife are of Italian descent and were enamored with the beautiful palazzos of Venice and Rome. They had collected Italian antiques on their trips to Italy—everything from Murano glass chandeliers to artwork—and realized what they really wanted was a home that reflected their love of Italy, something in which they could properly display their growing collection of antiques. Then the homeowners met Richard Loomis and David Herchik. The designers and homeowners understood each other immediately and it was not long afterwards that they began a five-year transformation of the home into a gracious and elegant Italian villa.

Trompe l'oeil frescos in pale green and pink based on Doge's Palace in Venice decorate the walls of the elegant parlor. Complementary curtains are designed in Nancy Corzine's light sage "Venetian Taffeta." Furniture is a mixture of Italian and French antiques, including the nineteenth-century French bow-front marquetry commode next to the window.

The parlor was designed after the Palazzo Ducale, or Doge's Palace, in Venice. Wall panels were faux painted with frescos in pale pink and green, based on the palace's woodwork. Furnishings included a mixture of French and Italian antiques, even a Steinway piano, which was hand gilded to match the room's décor. Curtains in Nancy Corzine's "Venetian Taffeta" in a light sage green were designed with classic swags and tails draped on gilded, carved rods. "Illusion" silk sheers, also from Nancy Corzine, were added underneath for privacy. Scalamandré's tan, green and gold silk-tassel trim was used to border both the panels and valance. The elegant room evokes a feeling of ancient gentility.

The dining room was inspired by the Florian, one of Venice's most famous cafés. Panels of hand-painted silvered tea paper were inset in the walls and accented with a mirrored silver commode by Julia Gray. Simple yet elegant curtains were designed in Brunschwig and Fils's "St. Petersburg Stripe" in a soft ivory and peony, gathered in Italian string panels. Nancy Corzine's "Illusion" in silk was again used for Austrian sheers underneath. Scalamandré's "Rose Quartz" beaded trim was added to etch the outlines of the draperies in soft pink. Dining chairs were found in Italy by the designers and upholstered in a silvery French blue-and-gold damask, also bought in Rome from the House of Rubelli. The room now sparkles like a precious gem in the muted colors of ancient Venice.

OPPOSITE: *The dining room walls sparkle with silver tea-leaf panels hand painted with designs from Venice's famed Florian Café. Italian string panels are "St. Petersburg Stripe" from Brunschwig and Fils.*

ABOVE: *Valances of "Venetian Taffeta," with classic swags and cascades, are hung on gilded rods with wreaths and acanthus leaf finials from Scalamandré. Austrian panels of silk sheers in "Illusion" are from Nancy Corzine.*

BELOW: *The pink-and-ivory silk curtain panels of "St. Petersburg Stripe" are accented with "Rose Quartz" beaded trim from Scalamandré.*

ABOVE: *The master bedroom is furnished with a gold, ivory and blue suite of bedroom furniture bought in Milan. Walls are painted a soft powdery blue and the windows are dressed with Italian string curtain panels in Brunschwig and Fils's "Blue Taffeta."*

OPPOSITE, TOP: *The daughter's bedroom is as sunny as an Italian afternoon with blue-and-yellow cotton chintz curtains in Cowtan and Tout's "Sweet Pea Trellis." The banquette was upholstered in a corresponding blue-and-white cotton, with accent pillows added in Scalamandré's sky and daffodil "Susan."*

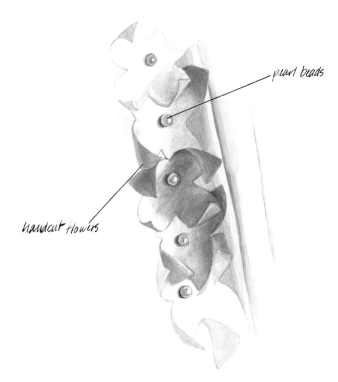

pearl beads

handcut flowers

The master bedroom upstairs was decorated around an elegant blue, ivory and gold dressing table and a suite of bedroom furniture the owners bought on their honeymoon in Milan. Walls were painted a soft powdery blue from Benjamin Moore and spectacular Italian string draperies were constructed in Brunschwig and Fils's "Blue Taffeta," their edges lined with silk taffeta flowers. Each flower was laboriously hand cut from Brunschwig and Fils's "Mansion Green" silk taffeta, stiffened with iron-on adhesive and its leaves given a curl around a pencil. A shiny pearl button was then sewn into the flower's center for the final touch.

The owners' oldest daughter's bedroom was made as bright and sunny as an Italian afternoon. The bay window that overlooks the gardens was draped with Cowtan and Tout's "Sweet Pea Trellis" in a sunny yellow-and-blue cotton chintz; a flat pull shade in the same fabric was added for privacy. A classic valance of swags and jabots was kept narrow to avoid obscuring the view. A curved banquette was designed for the bay in a complementary blue-and-white cotton, and pillows in Scalamandré's "Susan" cotton in daffodil and sky were added for cheerful accents. ◆

MARK GARRETT

Mark Garrett, born and raised in Nashville, Tennessee, has been involved in historic preservation and design for many years. He was the owner of Magnolia Hall, a famous Nashville-area plantation, and he operated a successful design business as well. Now based in San Francisco, Mark continues to work on projects in the South as well as the West Coast. An emphasis on classic design and antiques are trademarks appreciated by his clients across the country.

Modern-Day Nashville Plantation

No expense was spared for the construction of this grand, 30,000-square-foot home sited on fifty acres outside Nashville. A modern-day plantation, the home boasts classically inspired interiors with views of the sweeping lawns and gardens. The large rooms are perfect for entertaining and are furnished with a mixture of French and Italian antiques. Mark helped the owners select an apricot-and-green Old World Weavers damask for the dining room bay window. Formal swags and tails decorate the valance, which follows the curve of the bay window. Scalamandré's "Edward's Collection," an extravagant silk fringe, was added to the edges of the curtains and valance for an opulent touch. The kitchen window overlooking the backyard patio and fountain was finished with a silk-and-linen valance from Coraggio Textiles that was swagged over a painted pole. A pull-down shade in the matching fabric was added beneath for privacy. ◆

PREVIOUS OVERLEAF: *The formal dining room is furnished with beautiful eighteenth-century French and Italian antiques. The apricot-and-green damask curtains and swagged valance emphasize the classic formal look.*

LEFT: *Scalamandré's "Edward's Collection," an elegant silk fringe, was used to accent the leading edges of the curtain panels and valance.*

OPPOSITE: *The large and comfortable kitchen has a center island used for breakfast and quick meals. The window over the sink looks onto the backyard patio and fountain and is covered with a Coraggio Textile silk-and-linen blend that is elegantly swagged over a painted pole. A pull-down shade in the matching fabric can close out the world when privacy is desired.*

ABOVE: *The spacious living room boasts its original beamed ceiling and large picture window, which was updated with elegant panels and swagged cornice in Scalamandré's silk taffeta "Shangri-la" in shrimp cocktail.*

OPPOSITE: *Narrow side windows emphasize the arch of the ceiling. The curtains reflect their shape with panels of a silk taffeta stripe, "Shimmer Silk," from Scalamandré in shrimp. The trim is from Houlès.*

Mill Valley Remodel

The owners of this gracious Mill Valley, California, home had lived in it for more than two decades, enjoying its magnificent views of Sausalito and the ocean. However, the 1920s home was dark and cramped, so they embarked on a major remodel, bringing it into the present but preserving its vintage charm and the outstanding views.

The living room was updated, painted a warm russet "Downing Street Red" from ICI Paint; the original beamed ceiling was kept intact. Curtains were constructed for the large picture window in Scalamandré's silk taffeta "Shangri-la" in a warm shrimp cocktail pink. A corresponding silk taffeta stripe, "Shimmer Silk," in shrimp was used to cover the cornice board, which was then finished with elegant swags and tails. Narrow side windows looking towards the nearby mountains were covered with "Shimmer Silk," with simple smocked panels following the pointed outlines of the window frames. Filled with the owners' extensive collection of Lalique and other art glass, the living room is now a warm and inviting remodel of classic good design. ◆

Meredith Moriarty is not your typical decorator. A former high school English teacher and mother of three, Meredith decided to become a designer at the urging of friends and family. Meredith is blessed with an innate sense of proportion and design, perfect "color pitch" and, most importantly, a calmness that serves her clients well. Curtains are crucial in Meredith's interiors—they are like ball gowns she explains, detailed works of art.

English Charm
in Chicago

Meredith's clients had already gone through four previous decorators before they were referred to her. With five active children, they wanted a family-friendly home, something they could enjoy without worrying but that still had style and charm. Meredith knew exactly what they needed: an English country look, with classic, faded linens, simple and colorful toiles and furnishings that were well constructed and could hold up to large dogs and Jedi warriors.

The living room was made into a "room for living" with simple bump-lined curtains made from George Smith's "Blown Peonies" in a soft, floral linen and installed on hidden rings with custom poles and finials. A comfortable sofa and slipcovered club chairs from George Smith (all manufactured in England) added to the look of slightly faded English

The family-friendly living room is furnished with a comfortable sofa and slipcovered chairs from George Smith that hold up even to Duke, the family's 150-pound Burmese Mountain Dog. Simple panels of George Smith's "Blown Peonies" in a faded floral linen were constructed for the windows; the fabric is repeated in sofa cushions and the ottoman edge. A Clarence House cotton was used for both the slipcovers and curtain linings. The overall look is one of comfortable, worn-in English charm.

charm. The English country décor was carried over to the nearby breakfast room, where Cowtan and Tout's cheerful linen "Floral Blue Toile" was used at the leaded-glass windows. A contrast binding in a soft, blue check from Lee Jofa, "Belle Taffeta," helped define the curtains' edges.

Monogrammed linen slipcovers for the chairs in matching blue and white gave the room a tailored look and coordinated nicely with the owner's collection of blue-and-white china. Smart and comfortable, it's a breakfast room that works for the whole family. ◆

OPPOSITE: *The breakfast room's leaded glass windows are covered with Cowtan and Toutfis cheerful "Floral Blue Toile." The blue-and-white theme is repeated in custom monogrammed linen slipcovers on the chairs. Sunny and cheerful, the room is a favorite spot for breakfast for the busy family.*

ABOVE: *The breakfast room's curtains are light and sunny in Cowtan and Toutfis linen "Floral Blue Toile," accented with contrast binding in Lee Jofa's "Belle Taffeta" blue-and-white check.*

Combating Coldness with Color
in North Chicago

The owners of this large, historic Italianate in a Chicago suburb loved the scale and size of its rooms but not its coldness and stiff formality. Meredith helped them give it personality and playfulness with the simple addition of color in the living room and adjoining music room. Walls were painted a soft, summery yellow and colorful curtains were made with Scalamandré's bright, multicolored linen-and-silk "Dorset Plaid" in primary blue, yellow and red. The panels are accented with soft, folded-over pleats at the top. A sofa covered in Lee Jofa's red woven "Insecaire" (the pattern is crawling with little bugs), an ottoman upholstered in Nobilis's blue plaid "Anjou" and matching throw pillows all add life and playfulness to the formal parlor.

The adjoining music room was given a welcome jolt of color with blue walls and playful cotton shades made from Cowtan and Tout's "Harlequin." A wood mold was used to precisely cut out the bottom edge points, and then they were accented with Brunschwig and Fils's "Menuiserie" wood mold fringe for a finishing touch. ◆

LEFT: *The music room was jazzed up with bright blue walls and a multicolored window shade in Cowtan and Tout's "Harlequin." Notice the wooden mold fringe accents on the bottom points—just the right finishing touch.*

RIGHT: *The formal parlor is lightened with soft yellow walls and colorful curtain panels in Scalamandré's linen-and-silk "Dorset Plaid." An ottoman in a cheerful blue plaid from Nobilis-"Anjou"—and a sofa in Lee Jofa's strong red "Insecaire" all combine to make the room playful and inviting to the couple's small children and even Ruby, their patient yellow Lab.*

Master Bedroom
Make-over
in Chicago

A magazine ad is what started this master bedroom make-over in a comfortable North Chicago home. The owner saw Osborne and Little's woven cotton "Pomegranate Tree" in a magazine, fell in love with its large floral pattern and asked Meredith to design her master bedroom around it.

Meredith began by pulling the colors of the fabric in to the room—walls were glazed a warm, salmon-peach and the headboard was upholstered in Osborne and Little's "Fustian" in green. Custom gilded poles were ordered, with finials hand painted in coral and green. Meredith even found a hand-tufted McAdoo rug from Vermont, decorated with images of high heels—just the playful note she needed. Now a comfortable and inviting room, it's one in which the owner really can walk in and kick off her shoes. ◆

LEFT: *This master bedroom was designed around Osborne and Little's large-patterned "Pomegranate Tree." Soft salmon-peach glazed walls and coral and green accents make the room warm and inviting. The headboard is upholstered in Osborne and Little's "Fustian" green, and "Pomegranate Tree" is repeated on the bed's throw pillows. The framed photographs are of the owner's children in the 1950s.*

ABOVE: *Meredith's attention to detail is one of her keys to success. She had custom gilded curtain rods made with finials hand finished in coral and green to exactly match the colors of the fabric.*

Congresswoman's Curtains
in Chicago

A U.S. Congress member's home in western Chicago is one of the oldest in the area. An imposing Italianate, its large rooms boast details such as original molding and trim, wide window seats and large, glazed windows. Meredith has celebrated Christmas in this lovely home for more than thirty years, so when its owner asked her to help update the front parlor, Meredith was delighted.

As the congresswoman entertains frequently, Meredith chose a formal and elegant look. Clarence House's striped silk damask "Imberline Caserta" in soft corals, greens and yellows was chosen for the curtains, which were designed with classic swags, jabots and tails. Pink silk damask from Cowtan and Tout was used to upholster a pair of loveseats and add warmth. An ottoman was tufted in a soft gray strie velvet to double as a coffee table and extra seating. Elegant and still practical, the room is a perfect reflection of the owner's tastes and sensibilities. ◆

ABOVE: *The soft greens, corals and yellows of Clarence House's silk damask add a subtle note of color to the swagged valance over the window seat. The curtain trim was custom made in matching colors. The handsome dentil molding, which is original to the house, was deliberately kept uncovered.*

RIGHT: *The large, formal parlor was dressed with elegant curtain panels and valances in Clarence House's silk damask "Imberline Caserta" as the owner entertains frequently.*

ABOVE: *The hall curtains were lined with "Palm D'Or," a small check in cream and gold from Clarence House, and trimmed with "Dent de Rat," also from Clarence House.*

OPPOSITE: *The formal entrance hall was updated with glazed yellow-and-cream stripes on the walls and a marble floor. The curtains over the small hall window were constructed from Brunschwig and Fils's "Fleur de Lis" in a gold woven silk. A French recamier beneath the window sets the mood of French formality. The gilt bronze wall sconces are antiques from France.*

French Formality
along Lake Michigan

Some of the most beautiful homes in Chicago lie north of the city in the picturesque towns bordering Lake Michigan. One such house, a striking Art Deco mansion, still maintains its classic and well-proportioned interiors. The current owners are ardent Francophiles who wanted to preserve the character of their home while adding a note of classic French formality, something in keeping with the home's Art Deco origins.

Meredith began with the entrance hall, updating it with black-and-white marble flooring and glazing the walls with yellow and cream stripes. Brunschwig and Fils's "Fleur de Lis" in woven cream silk was chosen for the curtain over the small hall window, and Clarence House's "Palm D'Or," a subtle gold check, was used to line the panels. A French recamier was placed beneath the hall window and upholstered in an elegant cream-and-gold silk, "Moody Mansion" from Scalamandré.

The hall opens onto the large parlor that runs the length of the house. Centered on a long, curved bay window, the parlor is light and airy, with views onto the surrounding lawns and gardens. To subtly tie the hall and living room together, Meredith used "Palm D'Or" again for elaborately swagged curtains over the parlor's french doors. Valances were constructed with a central choux (rosette) reaching to the ceiling to balance the low sweep of the large bay window. "Palmetto," a complementary gold silk from Clarence House, was used

to upholster a pair of French bergeres, while a glazed cotton chintz—Brunschwig and Fils's "Campanula" in creams, greens and pinks—was chosen for the sofa to reflect the colors of the garden outdoors. Anchored by a hand-tufted cream-and-gold rug woven with a pattern of classic reeds and ribbons, the room is French and formal yet beckons with color and light. ◆

LEFT: *The long parlor opens off the entrance hall and looks onto the gardens and lawns. Elaborate valances and panels were constructed over the french doors. Meredith used "Palm D'Or" again for the draperies to tie the entrance hall and parlor together. Formal French furnishings were chosen, including a pair of French bergeres. A gold-and-cream carpet was custom woven in a reed and ribbon design to add to the French formality and to help anchor the room.*

ABOVE: *Elaborate draperies in Clarence House's "Palm D'Or" were designed for the french doors on either side of the bay window, with the central choux in the valance reaching the ceiling to balance the low sweep of the bay window. Details such as silk cording wrapped around each tail and heavy gold silk tassel fringe from Scalamandré add to the formal French look.*

Classic Chintz Comfort
in Chicago

Meredith has applied her sense of color and attention to detail in her own master bedroom in Chicago. Elegant, goblet-pleated curtains were constructed from Cowtan and Tout's "Jubilee Rose," a glazed cotton chintz and trimmed with a Scalamandré tassel fringe in cream, green and rose. Meredith lined the panels in Brunschwig and Fils's "Quadrillage," a cheerful plaid taffeta and used the dull side of a simple green cotton chintz from Lee Jofa for contrast binding. Bolsters and custom lampshades in the same taffeta along with the bedspread made from the glazed chintz all helped give the room a coordinated and inviting appeal. ◆

OPPOSITE: *The master bedroom is a cheerful and inviting room with Cowtan and Tout's yellow striped wallpaper and colorful curtains and bedspread made from their glazed cotton chintz "Jubilee Rose." A Brunschwig and Fils plaid taffeta, "Quadrillage," was used to line the curtains and bedspread as well as for bolsters and custom shades for the swing-arm reading lamps on either side of the bed.*

ABOVE: *Twisted green-and-pink silk cording accents the goblet pleats on the valance, which is in the colorful glazed chintz "Jubilee Rose" from Cowtan and Tout. It is highlighted by a subtle contrast binding in a dull green cotton chintz from Lee Jofa.*

PHIL HUGH SMITH

Phil Smith has been an interior designer in the Boston area for nearly four decades, specializing in historic and fine interiors with classic furnishings and antiques. Phil is a charter member of the American Society of Interior Designers of New England, and his advice to his clients is always simple: buy the best and you will not be disappointed.

Dorothy Adams designs residential interiors from New England to the Florida Keys. Her goal is to insure that her clients have an enjoyable experience and the final product reflects their vision.

Commonwealth Avenue Conservation

In 1995 designer Dorothy Adams was asked to restore this home and asked Phil Hugh Smith to assist her. Fortunately, the interiors had never been significantly altered. Original, ornately carved woodwork and gilded plasterwork was still intact in the main parlor overlooking Commonwealth Avenue, and the other principal rooms also remained unchanged. A delicate blue silk damask from Marvic Textiles was chosen for the parlor draperies to coordinate with the room's powder blue walls. Hung on custom-built, curved-and-gilded rods over the front bay window, the curtains and valance of swags and jabots were finished with gold silk tassel fringe from Scalamandré. Furnishings reflecting the owner's love of France—including Empire-style chairs and a pedestal adorned with regal gilded swans—were purposefully selected.

The parlor bay window overlooking Commonwealth Avenue is draped with Marvic Textiles' blue silk damask in classic swags and jabots for an elegant and timeless look. The French Empire armchairs are recovered in Scalamandré's blue silk "Napoleon Bee." The gold-leafed poles and shell finials were custom made to coordinate with the original plasterwork.

ABOVE: *The ornately gilded mantelpiece and mirror, original to the room, reflect the elegant draperies in the bay window. Gold tiles in the fireplace are also original to the house.*

OPPOSITE, TOP: *The master bedroom is centered on curtains from Lee Behren, a blue silk damask accented with a valance of classic swags and jabots. Chairs in coordinating velvets and a Tabriz Persian wool carpet tie the room together.*

OPPOSITE, BOTTOM: *The master bedroom draperies are hung from custom gilded poles. A pink-and-crystal Art Deco light fixture echoes the room's pastel palette.*

A pastel palette of light pink and blue was chosen for the master bedroom upstairs. Curtains in a soft blue silk damask from Lee Behren were accented with a valance of classic swags and jabots to correspond with the window treatment in the parlor below. A custom, multicolored tassel fringe from Scalamandré in tickle-pink, blue and rose was made to accent the curtains and coordinate with the light pink walls of the room. Comfortable Baker chairs upholstered in coordinating pastel velvets and a pink-and-blue Persian carpet were chosen to complement the feminine décor. ◆

Seaside Retreat

The owners of the Commonwealth Avenue mansion spend much of their time outside of Boston in a rambling seaside retreat perched on the rocks above the crashing waves of the Atlantic. Phil has restored the circa 1900 home's interiors, including the large library, to a classic and elegant decor. The owners are enthusiastic antique collectors and many of their favorite finds are displayed in the warm and inviting room.

Phil began with the coffered ceiling, covering it with gold-leafed tea paper for an opulent look. Walls were paneled in rich mahogany woodwork and an antique Persian carpet underfoot complements the deep burgundy and gold of the room's furnishings. Generous window seats afford vistas of the ocean and the home's surrounding gardens. Rather than obscure the views, Phil framed them with classical Empire swags and tails constructed from Scalamandré's silk lampas "Rosecliff," whose design is based on a historic fabric from the Newport mansion of the same name. Gilded, custom-fabricated curtains rods and ram's-head finials complete the look for a warm and masculine retreat. ◆

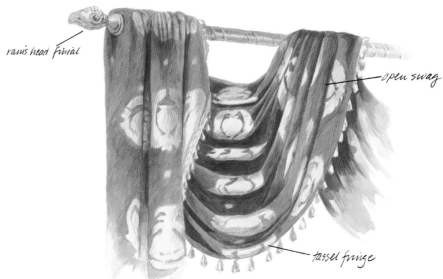

ram's head finial

open swag

tassel fringe

LEFT: *The waterfront home's library is warm and inviting. The coffered ceiling is papered in gold-leaf tea paper and its walls are paneled in rich mahogany. Furniture is a mixture of comfortable seating, such as the pair of button-tufted sofas upholstered in burgundy velvet. The owners, who are avid antiques collectors, have furnished the library with some of their favorites.*

ABOVE: *Custom-made finials in the form of rams' heads add an appropriately masculine touch to the library's curtain rods.*

OPPOSITE: *Wide window seats are covered in Scalamandré's silk lampas "Rosecliff," based on a design from the historic Newport mansion of the same name. Simple Empire swags and tails of the same fabric frame the views from the windows. Trim is a custom Scalamandré burgundy-and-gold silk tassel fringe. Gold-and-black accent pillows and a throw are made from Versace silks.*

Nashville is known for its country music and welcoming Southern hospitality. Its gracious hostesses enjoy creating elegant interiors, and well-designed draperies are an integral part. Scot Robbins runs one of the city's best window fabrication studios and has constructed custom window treatments for homes throughout the area. Also a frequent lecturer around the country, Scot teaches classes on curtain design and workroom techniques. Scot's expertise is evident when you view his work. His words of advice? Never sacrifice quality, he counsels, and the results will speak for themselves.

Dining Room Drama
in Tennessee

Working with design consultant Crystal Mowery from Calico Corners in Nashville, Scot helped overcome design challenges in an elegant and dramatic dining room. The homeowner wanted a formal and gracious window treatment for the room to complement her traditional décor, but, as Scot explained, the design was hampered by the limited amount of space (merely three inches) between the arched top of the dining room window and the heavy ceiling trim.

Scot solved the dilemma by custom designing arched cornice boards that were built out into the room to create a concave effect. Rich, mocha silk from Silk Loom was shirred over the cornice for a soft, smooth look. Drapery panels in the same silk were lined with three additional layers for a full and luxurious draping of the fabrics, in a technique known as "French Blackout": a layer of mocha silk followed by a layer of heavy, English bump flannel interlining, a third layer of black sateen and then a final layer of Prima sateen in ivory.

Three central swags were accented by cascades on each side of the cornice. Two drapery panels were employed—an outer, shorter length tied back to enhance the full floor-length panel underneath. Chocolate bullion fringe and tassel trim from Tuscany Imports' "Trivoli Collection" provide the finishing touches. The curtains complete the dining room perfectly, making it rich and dramatic—exactly what the homeowner wanted. ◆

LEFT: *Chocolate fringe and tassel trim from Tuscany Imports' "Trivoli Collection" line the edges of the swags and curtain panels.*

OPPOSITE: *Dramatic mocha brown silk from Silk Loom was used to construct the elaborate swagged valance and panels in this elegant Southern dining room. Four layers work together in the design: the silk drapery panels, an interlining of English bump flannel, a layer of black sateen and a final layer of Prima ivory sateen, for draperies that hang and drape beautifully.*

English Country Elegance

in Tennessee

Built in the softly rolling hills outside of Nashville, this large and inviting home was designed by the owners based on grand country houses they had visited in England. The homeowner furnished it with an engaging mix of antiques and custom-designed furniture, consulting Scot for simple yet elegant draperies in the dining room, which features twelve-foot-tall windows that flood the room with afternoon sunlight. Striped silk panels of iridescent gold and cranberry ("Onyx Age" from Calico Corners) were chosen, and Scot lined them with three additional layers of fabric in the "French Blackout" technique with the "Onyx Age" silk, followed by heavy flannel interlining, followed by black sateen, and finally a fourth layer of Prima ivory sateen. Simple, flip-over valances and "Euro" pleats make a handsome and straightforward design. Furnished with family antiques, the room is warm and welcoming—very much in the tradition of an English country manor. ◆

OPPOSITE: *Twelve-foot windows flood the dining room with afternoon sun. Scot designed simple yet elegant draperies in the gold and cranberry stripes of "Onyx Age," a silk from Calico Corners. Furnishings include a 1930s mahogany dining table (a family heirloom), a collection of antique leaded-glass decanters and Oriental figurines, for a personal, eclectic look. Host and hostess chairs flanking either side of the window are hand painted with inlay by Rho of Italy and upholstered with "Berrabamo," an Italian silk damask.*

ABOVE: *"Euro" pleats complete the simple yet elegant valance.*

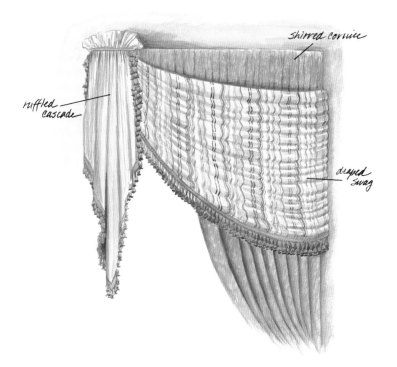

ruffled cascade

shirred cornice

drayed swag

Victorian Restoration
in Franklin, Tennessee

Franklin, Tennessee, is a picturesque, historic town near Nashville that was founded in the late eighteenth century. Blocks of meticulously restored homes line its streets, including this charming Victorian, which was built in 1898. Originally it was a simple cottage, but over the twelve years the owners have lived here, they have been slowly returning it to a complementary nineteenth-century elegance.

Scot was asked by designer Beth Rhora to help construct asymmetrical mirrored treatments for the two narrow dining room windows. Cornice boards were built and shirred in bronze colored "Daylily," a floral silk from Intex. Swags and jabots in Artee Silk's "Rama Satin Stripe" in gold and sage were added to the cornice, the swag hung lower on the cornice to reveal the shirred fabric beneath. Drapery panels of "Daylily" were tied to the sides to enhance the asymmetric effect. Gold "Treasure" tassel fringe from World Wide Trim was added to the borders of the valance swags and jabots as well as the curtain panels for just the right finishing touch. Furnished with antiques, including an extensive collection of Waterford crystal and vintage china, the room now exudes an air of nineteenth-century gentility and grace.

OPPOSITE: *The dining room's two windows are asymmetrically draped for more visual impact. The cornices are shirred in bronze "Daylily" silk from Intex, and the same fabric is repeated for the curtain panels. Swags and jabots of sage and gold "Rama Satin Stripe" from Artee Silk are the perfect complementary accents, repeating the colors of the carpet. Antique furnishings include a mahogany sideboard and dining table. Dining chairs are upholstered in "Neosho Gold Bronze" cotton blend.*

ABOVE: *Swags of multicolored "Rama Satin Stripe," a silk from Artee Silk, are finished with gold "Treasure" tassel fringe from World Wide Trim.*

The owner, an admitted flea market junkie, has let her passion run rampant in her colorful kitchen. Furnished with flea market treasures from ceramic roosters to an amusing, carved "Smoked Salmon" smoking a cigar, the kitchen brings a smile to everyone who enters. Beth had simple cotton panels fabricated by Bonnie Kinion in Magnolia's "Palisades" in a warm spearmint, red and tan, banding the bottom edges with a matching burgundy textured cotton. The owner, of course, provided vintage swing-arm tiebacks she had found on a flea market forage. ◆

LEFT: *The kitchen reflects the owner's passion for flea markets and collecting. Simple curtains over the window are constructed in "Palisades," a cotton in spearmint, red and tan, and accented with a bottom banding in burgundy textured cotton. The smoking Smoked Salmon was found by the owner.*

ABOVE: *Polychromed, ca. 1920s swing-arm tiebacks hold back the kitchen curtains. The soft green, red and tan colors of the curtains are a good complement to the owner's collections of colorful vintage ceramics and kitchenware.*

Susan Lamy has been a successful interior designer for more than twenty years. Based in Connecticut, she designs beautiful homes around the country in a wide variety of styles. Susan has a penchant for French décor—she used to own a French antiques shop, designed her own line of country French fabrics and is married to a Frenchman, mais oui. Her creative and beautiful window treatments have won many awards. As Susan explains, curtains are among the first details you notice when you enter a room, and are what make a room feel finished and complete.

Connecticut Traditional
with a Twist

Susan's clients for this rambling, comfortably updated Victorian in pastoral Connecticut have four active children, so wanted a family room that would be the center of the house. Open to both the kitchen and a dinette eating bay, the space needed to be functional yet colorful and inviting. Susan began with the bright blues and pinks in the Oriental rug and created a rosy bower with Scalamandré's floral cotton "Gertrude's Rose" for the windows. The flowers run upwards in the fabric's pattern; to emphasize this, she created unique cornices that have the flowers growing right up through their tops. "Gertrude's Rose" was used for a complementary shirred valance in the dinette area, and the bottom cornices for both windows were trimmed with the cheerful blue pom-pom balls of "Bobble Fringe" from Cowtan and Tout. A window seat was also enlivened with a shirred valance, as were cushions in the same fabric in the adjacent hall. Swivel Pearson Furniture club chairs and a custom Charles Stewart ottoman were covered in Scalamandré's chenille "Paulette" in alternating blush red and powder blue for the family seating area. Traditional, comfortable and surprisingly colorful, this family room has become just what the owners hoped for. The curtains have attracted much admiration

A bower of roses in pinks and blues sets the theme of the family room with draperies in Scalamandré's cotton floral "Gertrude's Rose." Pink-and-blue "Paulette" chenilles from Scalamandré continue the colorful theme in the upholstered ottoman and chairs.

and were even awarded Connecticut Home book's Golden Award, their highest honor.

The dining room was designed around an antique mahogany table and chairs from Charles Stewart that were upholstered in alternating viscose and cotton jacquards from Pierre Frey. Generous pencil-pleated window panels were made from Stroheim and Romann's "Dresden" silk taffeta plaid and hung on carved wooden poles finished in matching silver leaf finials and tiebacks. Lined in faux silk, the panels puddle luxuriantly on the floor and add to the room's opulent feel. The adjacent bay window was also dressed in "Dresden," with an Empire-style valance. The walls are painted pale pink and give the room a warm, inviting glow—traditional, but with a twist of unexpected color and design. ◆

OPPOSITE, TOP: *Roses were laboriously cut out by hand for the valances to give the impression they were growing out of the fabric. Blue pom-pom fringe from Cowtan and Tout, "Bobble Fringe," is a whimsical accent.*

OPPOSITE, BELOW: *Pillows in Scalamandré's "Gertrude's Rose" soften the wide window seat, one of the owners' favorite features in the Victorian home.*

ABOVE: *A cozy window seat blooms with roses, with a flat valance and cushions in "Gertrude's Rose."*

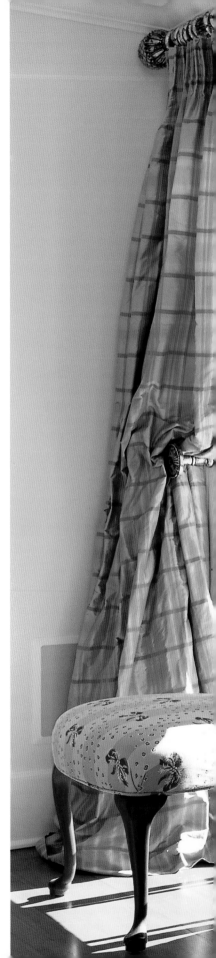

ABOVE: *The dining room glows with warm, soft pink walls and the golden tones of "Dresden" silk taffeta draperies from Stroheim and Romann. The Stark carpet was custom designed for the room in an octagonal shape to highlight the round eighteenth-century dining table. Dining room chairs are upholstered in alternating jacquards in floral pinks and aqua blues from Pierre Frey.*

RIGHT: *The silk taffeta dining room drapes glow in the afternoon sun. Lined in a faux silk, the panels are generously gathered into pencil pleats and puddled on the floor for a luxurious look. Note the pole finials and tiebacks, which are highlighted with silver leaf.*

Understated
Old-World Elegance
in Connecticut

The owners of this Connecticut home asked Susan to help them furnish it with old-world elegance but in an understated manner. Susan chose rich, jewel-toned color schemes for the main rooms to complement inherited family antiques. The dining room was designed around the clients' striking dining table, a family heirloom that features an unusual marble top. The soft greens and peachy apricot colors of the marble were used as a color guide for faux finishing the walls and woodwork.

The living room bay is finished with curtains in "Grimaldi," a Jab silk in gold stripes. Contrast lining in the rich claret red of Robert Allen's "Dalliance" is a warm and inviting touch. The Louis XV center table from Julia Gray features intricate ormolu inlay. The reproduction Louis XV fauteuils are upholstered in "Fontanelle," a gold-and-burgundy silk stripe from Grey Watkins, to complement the gold-and-claret curtains. The room is a like a glowing jewel box.

Window treatments were designed for simplicity and scale, constructed in "Callaway," a faux silk from Artmark, using a board-mounted pelmet with a kick pleat at the center and slight shirring at the corners and returns. Drapery panels were pinch pleated and interlined for proper weight and draping, and contrast lining in a matching gold silk taffeta from Michael's Textiles was added. Louis XV–style dining chairs were upholstered in Nobilis's "Leonie," a green-and-gold cotton with embroidered floral stripes; their backs were covered in the coordinating large checked "Leon." An Empire chandelier provided the finishing touch of old-world elegance and understated charm.

The living room was faux finished in a mix of gold and ochre tones to create a glowing jewel box. Draperies were kept simple while constructed in luxurious fabrics for understated elegance. Hung from simple, classic brass rods, the curtain panels were constructed from a Jab silk, "Grimaldi," in warm, tone-on-tone gold stripes, goblet pleated and then contrast lined with Robert Allen's "Dalliance" in rich claret red. A pair of reproduction Louis XV French fauteuils in the bay window were upholstered in "Fontanelle," a gold-and-burgundy silk stripe from Grey Watkins that complements the draperies. Warm and inviting, the living room is an elegant example of the importance of color in a well-designed room. ◆

OPPOSITE: *The owner's heirloom dining table with an unusual marble top provided the theme for the elegant dining room. Colors in the tabletop are repeated in faux finishes on the walls and woodwork. The window treatments are purposefully simple yet elegant, constructed in "Callaway," a faux silk plaid from Artmark.*

ABOVE: *A sparkling Empire crystal chandelier is highlighted against the dining room draperies. Pinch pleated, interlined and then contrast lined with gold silk taffeta from Michael's Textiles, they are an understated yet elegant focal point.*

French Country Manor
in New Hampshire

The owners of this comfortable home in New Hampshire, a "smart" house with all the advantages of modern technology—from an elevator to a heated driveway to melt the heavy New Hampshire ice and snow—wanted a warm and sophisticated decor, something with the feeling of an inviting French country manor. Susan chose her favorite color of French blue as the starting point, using different shades and tones in each room for a cheerful, country appeal, while keeping the different rooms coordinated throughout the house. In the garden room Susan added accents of purples and greens to the bright Provençal blues, while in the dining room and master bedroom blues and creamy whites predominate. The soaring two-story family room was enlivened with yellow accents to the blue-and-cream color scheme. Even the hallways were painted in coordinating blue-and-cream stripes to connect the flow of space between the rooms. Smart and tailored, the home now exudes the charm of Provence but with the practicality of today.

The garden room at the end of the house is a striking octagonal space, with windows overlooking the gardens on all sides and light pouring in from an overhead cupola. Susan upholstered the walls in Manual Canovas' spring-like blue-green-and-white floral cotton print "Amita" and constructed

ABOVE: *Sheffield window valances in "Amita" from Manual Conavas are lined in a matching blue-and-white cotton check from Duralee and trimmed with a contrast welt in the same fabric.*

RIGHT: *The octagonal garden room is bright and sunny, with curtains made from "Amita," a blue-green-and-white cotton print from Manual Conavas and walls upholstered in the same fabric. Purple accents such as the embroidered hydrangeas on the camel-back slipper chairs around the center stone table highlight the bright, Provençal blue of the woodwork.*

Sheffield window valances in the same fabric, lining and contrasting them with a coordinating blue-and-white cotton check from Duralee. Pinch pleated side panels reaching the floor envelope the room in a delightful bower. Woodwork was painted a bright Provençal blue ("Celeste" from Pratt and Lambert) and the brick floor was painted white and embellished with a hand-drawn frieze of flowers taken from the draperies. Furniture was selected to complement the colors of the curtains, with "Annabelle" loveseats upholstered in Stroheim and Romann's blue-and-white "St. Bart's Stripe" and a pair of Montgolfiere chairs upholstered in Cowtan and Tout's blue-and-white "Larkfield Check," an embroidered cotton. A stone-topped center table for dining was found, and camel-back slipper chairs upholstered in a silk-and-linen weave from Berger were chosen, making it the perfect spot for morning croissants and café au lait.

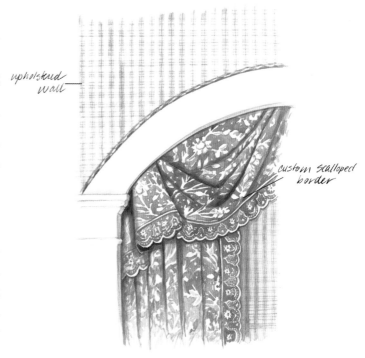

The dining room is Susan's "dream come true." Walls were upholstered in "Trompette," a blue-and-white cotton chintz check from Nobilis. Dining room chairs were upholstered in the same cotton check for a coordinated look.

Exquisite window treatments were created from Brunschwig and Fils's "Verrieres" cotton floral chintz. Swagged Empire valances were edged with a scalloped border cut from the chintz; the elegant, scalloped swags continue into an arched niche at the end of the room, which holds a custom-painted Louis Quinze reproduction buffet. Susan admits her window workroom was not enthralled with the laborious project of hand cutting the many yards

RIGHT: *The dining room is a symphony in blue and white, with "Trompette," a chintz check from Nobilis, on the walls and dining chairs upholstered in the same fabric. "Verrieres," a floral cotton from Brunschwig and Fils, was used for the drapery panels and swagged valance, which is accented with a scalloped border laboriously cut by hand from the fabric. The elegant treatment was carried over to the arched cornice at the end of the room. A blue-and-white custom carpet from Stanton Carpet—"Yardley," with "Lismore" border—was selected to help anchor the room.*

OPPOSITE: *The blue-and-white swags and panels of "Verrieres," from Brunschwig and Fils, are highlighted with a scalloped border cut from the fabric. The room's mixture of multiple blue-and-white patterns works beautifully for an elegant, sophisticated look.*

156 ✒ SUSAN LAMY

of scalloped chintz, but everyone agreed the end result was well worth the effort. The room now sparkles, a tour de force of French blue-and-white sophistication.

The owners have four young children and had never taken the time to decorate their bedroom. They asked Susan to make their master suite their own special romantic and private retreat. Walls were upholstered in Brunschwig and Fils's blue-and-cream "Manon," a floral cotton print, for quiet and privacy; soundproofing was reinforced with a coordinating custom Brugge area rug with an Antwerp border. The four-poster canopied bed was hand painted in blue and cream and hung with Cowtan and Tout's embroidered silk "Marissa Sheer" for a dreamy and seductive look.

Window treatments needed to be light and pretty while completely shutting out light for privacy. Susan selected Cowtan and Tout's silk-and-linen, blue-and-cream "Sarvana Stripe," and repeated it in the pillow shams and dust ruffle on the bed. The drapery panels were lined and interlined to eliminate unwanted light and roller shades laminated in the wall cotton print "Manon" were added. Elegant valances with goblet pleats and contrasting cream buttons were installed. The room is now a fairy-tale retreat fit for a prince and princess.

The family room is the heart of the house, open to the kitchen and the center of activity for the family's active young children. The family often enjoys meals at the dining table overlooking the back gardens. The large, two-story Palladian window was dressed with swags of Artee's blue-and-yellow floral linen-and-cotton print "China Rose Georgianna," held with a center rosette. Flat Roman shades were installed on the side windows and on french doors in the same fabric for control of the afternoon sun. Walls were painted a sunny ochre with an undercoat of blue to give the feeling of ancient, Venetian plaster. ◆

OPPOSITE, TOP: *The master bedroom is upholstered in Brunschwig and Fils's "Manon," which is repeated on roller shades. Curtains are constructed with Cowtan and Tout's "Sarvana Stripe" in blues and cream and accented with goblet pleats. Blue-and-white bed coverings include the coverlet, which is made from F. Schumacher's "Isabel Embroidered Matalasse" with a reverse sham top. The pillows and coverlet shams are ruffled in Cowtan and Tout's "Sarvana Stripe" to coordinate with the draperies and dust ruffle. Bed curtains from Cowtan and Tout's delicate linen-and-silk embroidered "Marissa Sheer" were shirred from the bed canopy.*

OPPOSITE, BOTTOM: *Detail of the bedroom draperies shows the goblet-pleated valance accented with contrasting cream buttons. The drapery panels are lined and interlined to shut out the light and provide privacy.*

RIGHT: *The family room is lit by a large, two-story Palladian window. Artee's "China Rose Georgianna," a blue-and-yellow linen and cotton, was swagged across the upper arches and repeated in Roman blinds on the french doors and windows below. Ochre walls give the room a sunny and welcoming appearance.*

Glossary of Terms

The main terms that are defined—not preceded by aka (also known as)—are the accepted and approved terms of the WCAA. All aka terms indicate that the industry sometimes uses them interchangeably with the accepted terms.

Allowance: A customary variation from an "exact" measurement, taken for the purpose of anticipated needs.

Apron: The wood trim molding below the windowsill.

Appliqué: To sew or fuse a piece of cut out cloth to another piece of cloth. Also the term used for the piece of cloth applied.

Austrian shade: A fabric shade known for its formal appearance and vertical shirring between the scallops. Usually made of sheer fabric and classified as a sheer under treatment.

Austrian valance: A soft, stationary valance fabricated like the Austrian shade, with the vertical rows of shirred fabric that form a scalloped bottom edge.

Back tack: (aka backstitch) Stitching at the beginning or the end of the seam done by stitching backwards and forwards in order to lock and secure the seam.

Balloon shade: A type of fabric shade known for the permanent poufs that form at the bottom of the shade as the shade is raised. It has permanent poufs in it when it is down as well. The heading may be any type of heading as long as your fabric has the correct fullness. Some examples are: box pleated, gathered or smocked.

Balloon valance: A soft, stationary valance fabricated like the balloon shade that is known for the poufs at the bottom edge.

Bar-tack: A sewing machine operation of repeated stitches concentrated to secure the lowest portion of drapery pleats.

Baton: A rod or wand used to hand draw traverse draperies.

Bay window: A group of windows set at angles to each other.

Bed skirt: (aka dust ruffle) A skirt that covers the box springs of the mattress and the bed frame.

Bendable lauan: (aka Wiggle Board) Bendable plywood usually ripped into return sizes and used for arched treatments. It can also be used to form a curved face on cornices and coronas.

Bias cut: Fabric cut that is 45-degree angle of the fabric weave. This cut of fabric will have give to it, allowing swags to drape better, and better enable cording to hug curves. Prints should be checked before cutting on the bias. Some upright prints can be cut on the bias and look great, others can't.

Board line: The line drawn on the pattern pieces to indicate where the treatment will be placed at the front edge of the board.

Bottom hem: The turned part forming a finished edge at the bottom of drapery.

Boston edge: (aka micro cord) 1.8 mm welt cord.

Bowed cornice: A cornice with convex or concave curves on the face.

Bow window: A type of window that is curved or semi-circular.

Box pleat: Pleats formed by two folded edges facing each other. Box pleats are evenly spaced and stitched.

A. Closed box pleat: Pleats of fabric are pressed flat so the edges of the pleats touch each other all the way across the front and all the way across the back of the treatment (three times fullness).

B. Open box pleat: Pleats of fabric are taken on the front of the treatment and pressed flat against the front but there is a space between the edges of the pleats on the front.

C. Inverted box pleats: Pleats of fabric are taken in the back of the treatment and pressed flat against the back but the sides do not touch.

Bullion fringe: A long, thick fringe of individual cords or twisted cords.

Break: The extra length added to draperies so they lay on the floor 1 inch to a few inches.

Breaking the buckram: The practice of creasing the buckram between pleats in order to make the pleats fall properly when draperies are opened. Usually done at installation.

Buckram: See "crinoline."

Café: A traversing or non-traversing short drapery, designed as a tier, with various heading styles.

Café rod: A small, round decorative rod used to mount café curtains that do not have a rod pocket. Café rods are meant to be seen and add a decorative touch to the window treatment.

Canopy: A fabric bed treatment that goes over the top of a specialty bed frame.

Cantonniere: A three-sided, shaped or straight cornice that "frames" the window across the top and part way down the two sides. It is usually made of hardboard, padded and covered with fabric.

Carriers: (aka slides) Small runners installed in the traverse rod, which hold a drapery pin or hook.

Cartridge pleat: A fold of cloth sewn into place to create fullness in a drapery. This is a round pleat 2 to 2 1/2 inches in depth. Stuffing the pleat with buckram that may be removed for cleaning creates a round shape.

Blind hemming an Arts and Crafts curtain panel is done by turning back the hem to the wrong side and stitching a seam.

Cascade: (aka tails) Often used with swags, a fall of knife-pleated fabric that descends in a zigzag line from the drapery heading or top treatment. They should be self- or contrast lined.

Casement:

A. Fabric: A cloth drapery that is an open-weave material but more opaque than a sheer.

B. Window: A type of vertically hinged window, whose panes open by sliding sideways or cranking outward.

Casing:

A. Fabric: A pocket made in fabric for a curtain rod, weight board or drawstring.

B. Window: A wooden frame around the window.

Center draw: (aka split draw) A traversing pair of draperies that draw open from and close to a window's center point.

Center support: A piece of hardware that supports a traverse rod from above to prevent the rod from sagging, yet does not interfere with the rod operation. A wood or metal support is used for poles and metal rods that do not traverse; they are supported from underneath the rod.

Chain weights: A continuous chain of small heavy beads covered in a casing, used to prevent billowing in lightweight fabric.

Clearance: Distance from the back of the rod/pole to the wall.

Clerestory windows: A series of small windows that let in light and air, usually high up on the wall to allow privacy.

Cloud shade: Similar to a balloon shade, forms poufs at the bottom of the treatment as the shade is raised but the bottom is straight across when it is down.

Cloud valance: A stationary top treatment similar to the cloud shade that cannot be raised or lowered.

Comforter: A bed covering without a pillow-tuck that is usually a throw style and does not cover the entire bedsides—it covers the mattress plus 3 or 4 inches on the sides and foot of the bed.

Concave curve: An inward curve (a bow window has an inward curve).

Contrast lining: A decorative fabric used as a lining or decking when parts of it may show from the front of the top treatment.

Convex curve: An outward curve.

Cording: (aka welt cord) A rope that is covered with fabric, also referred to as piping or welting.

Cord cleat: A piece of hardware attached to the wall around which window treatment cords can be secured. (As a safety precaution use these to keep the cords out of children's reach.)

Cord lock: A piece of hardware mounted to the head rail of a shade, through which the operating cords run. When the cords are pulled up, it secures the shade at the desired location.

Cornice: A box treatment usually constructed of wood that can be padded and upholstered.

C.O.M.: (aka COM) Customer's own material.

Coverlet: A bedcovering with a pillow tuck and a short drop that covers the mattress but not the box springs. This is usually used in conjunction with a bed skirt.

Crinoline: (aka buckram) A heavily sized or stiff fabric used as a foundation for pleats in draperies.

Crosswise grain: (aka fillers, woof, weft) The threads of a woven fabric that run perpendicular to the selvages. The fabric has a slight give in the crosswise grain.

Custom-made draperies: Draperies made to order in a workroom or decorator shop.

Cut allowance: The amount of fabric added to finished measurements for hems and headings.

Cut length: (aka cut) The length of the fabric cut after allowances have been added for heading, hem and repeats.

Cutout Return: A buttonhole or rectangular cut out at the top return of the panel or top treatment to allow the return to go back to the wall in a pole-mounted treatment.

Cut width: The complete amount of fabric needed for treatment width, including hems, and/or any other allowances.

Decking:

A. Top Treatments: A contrast or self-fabric sewn to the bottom of the top treatment and pressed to the back to form a hem. This should be used when parts of the backside of the treatment may show from the front view.

B. Bed Skirts: The fabric that covers the box springs on a dust ruffle or bed skirt and to which the bed skirt is attached.

Decorative hardware: Hardware (such as swag holders, rods, poles, tiebacks rings) that can add aesthetic appeal to a window fashion as well as serve functional purposes.

Dormer window: An upright window that breaks the surface of a sloping roof.

Double hem: Folding the fabric over twice in equal amounts. A 4-inch double hem would utilize 8 inches of fabric.

Double hung draperies: Two sets of draperies, usually a sheer fabric under an opaque fabric, both operating separately.

Double top heading: This heading is commonly used for both pinch pleat and rod pocket draperies, where the heading has another full layer of fabric under the visible layer on the backside.

Drapery: Proper name for a long window covering, i.e., pinch-pleated drapery.

Drapery hardware: Functional hardware that is either used to support hard or soft window fashions (such as traverse rods, rings, hooks, etc.) or to support other hardware (such as end brackets, angle irons, pulleys, etc.).

Draw draperies: Panels of fabric that will open and close, usually on a traverse rod.

Draw-up: (aka take up) The loss in measurement as a result of the method of mounting and/or fabrication. This usually happens when gathering fabric on a rod.

Drop: A term for length commonly used in reference to valances.

Drop match: A drop-match is one in which the width is cut straight across by the print, but the print at the selvages will not line up perfectly to be seamed and hang straight. Therefore, additional yardage is required. Add one repeat per cut.

Dropped dust board cornice: A cornice with a decorative top that sometimes requires the dust board to be lower than usual. (Some workrooms use this method with arched top cornices.)

Dust board: The portion of the mount board or cornice to which the legs and/or the face are attached.

Duvet: A non-decorative throw style comforter designed to be used with a decorative removable cover.

Duvet cover: A slipcover for a removable comforter or duvet.

Elbow ends: Added to a wood pole, metal or PVC, this section is a continuation of the same shape that will turn the corner, providing the return and support. Sometimes called the elbow bracket.

End bracket: The two supporting pieces of hardware, which hold a drapery rod to the wall or ceiling. End brackets control the amount of projection.

End housing: Refers to the box parts at the extreme ends of a

A professional iron is a much-used tool in the workroom. A boiler is attached to the wall and water under pressure provides steam to the iron. Here Bortenfix iron-on tapes are used for matching patterns, banding and trims.

traverse drapery rod. They enclose the pulleys through which the cords run.

Envelope fold: A method of folding banding for application. The 1/2-inch seam allowance is pressed down on one side only. The remainder of the band is then folded double with the remaining raw edge going under the 1/2-inch seam allowance to meet the fold to create the finished width.

Euro pleat: A free-flowing drapery pleat with or without crinoline that has either two or three folds and is tacked within 1/2 inch from the top.

Eyebrow window: Arched top window with elongated width. Not a true half circle.

Fabrication: The process of manufacturing raw goods into a finished product.

Face fabric: The decorative fabric on a treatment that "faces" into the room. The lining is behind it.

Facing: A piece of fabric is stitched to a raw edge and turned to the backside to form a finished edge. The diagonals of jabots or cascades are sometimes faced to show a contrast in the angles.

False cord: (aka flat welt or flat trim) A flat, folded fabric stitched in the seam the same as a welt cord, minus the cord.

This gives you the look of welt, without the bulk.

Fan folded: A back-and-forth fold, like an accordion. Pinch pleated draperies are folded this way by folding pleat to pleat. This helps to train the folds of the drapery and makes handling the drapery easier and neater for installation.

Flat roman shade: A tailored fabric shade that hangs flat at the window. Soft pleats form at the bottom as the shade is raised.

Finial: Decorative ends of a pole, usually ornamental and affixed to the ends of a rod, which serve to keep drapery rings from falling off the rod.

Finished length: This is the length after draperies have been made.

Finished width: The actual width after the treatment is finished.

Flame retardant fabric: Fabric that will not burn. It can be inherently flame retardant which means the actual fiber from which it was made is a flame retardant fiber, e.g., polyester, or be treated to become flame retardant, which usually changes the fibers and makes the fabric stiff.

French pleat: see "Pinch pleat."

Front width: The width of the valance board without returns.

Fullness: The amount of extra fabric added to a finished measurement to create the desired "full" effect. The standard custom finish is 2 1/2 to 3 times the total width of a treatment.

Gathered roman shade: Shade made by shirring fabric onto horizontal ribs before assembling as a working roman shade.

Glass curtains: An old term for the draperies underneath draw draperies or stationary panels, known today as sheers.

Goblet pleat: (cartridge pleat with bottom tack) A fold of cloth sewn into place to create fullness in a drapery. This is a round pleat 2 to 2 1/2 inches in depth and tacked or pinched at the bottom. Stuffing made from tissue, Dacron or similar material that can be removed for cleaning may be inserted into the pleat in order to maintain the round or "goblet" shape.

Griege goods: Fabrics, regardless of color, that have been woven on a loom and have received no wet or dry finishing applications. Some griege goods have names such as "print cloth" and "soft-filled sheeting," which are used only for the griege goods. Other griege goods' names, such as "lawn," "broadcloth" and "sateen," are also used as names for the finished cloth.

Half-drop match: One in which the pattern itself drops down half the repeat. When the width is cut straight across by the print, the selvages will NOT match. Half the repeat on the opposite side will match. Additional yardage must be added.

Header: The ruffle edge that extends above a rod pocket.

Heading: The way a treatment is finished at the top, for example rod pocket draperies can have single or double tops. Also a decorative element, i.e., smocked heading.

Head-rail: The "board" to which shades are attached. The size is given according to the measurement of the return.

Hem: Refers to finished sides and bottom edges of a drapery.

Hidden single top: (pillow-cased) A type of buckram heading for pinch pleat draperies where the lining goes all the way to the top of the heading. There are 4 inches of face fabric and lining covering the buckram inside the panel.

Hobbled: (aka Soft Fold) A roman shade with permanent soft folds all the way up the shade.

Holdbacks: A decorative piece of hardware used to hold back draperies or hold up swags.

Hook and loop tape fastener (Velcro): Composed of two tape strips, one with a hook nap and the other with a loop nap. When pressed together they grip firmly to each other.

Horn: Smooth tapered portion of a top treatment that resembles a horn or bell shape. It can be made and attached separately or sewn in.

Hourglass curtain: A curtain panel anchored top and bottom and pulled tight in the middle with a tieback to reveal a triangular area of light on either side.

Inside measurement: Measurement for a treatment so the window facing would be exposed after the treatment is installed.

Inside mount: (ISM) Location of hardware and treatment are inside a structure, usually a window frame or cornice board.

Pins are synonymous with sewing. These pins are professional "Glass Head" pins from Germany and are favored for their strength and longer length. Old-fashioned pin cushions have pretty much been replaced by modern magnetic pin bowls.

Silk threads in every color of the rainbow are used in the workroom.

Mounting a treatment wall to wall is also treated as an inside mount.

Interfacing: A stiff fabric that is either sewn or fused on to give body to fabrics.

Interlining: A soft flannel-like fabric put between the face fabric and lining of draperies to add luxurious body as well as insulation. Interlinings add to a quality look, give weight, protect from fading and help to insulate. Interlining also comes in heavier weights called bump and table felt.

Jabots: (aka pelmets) Additional, optional pieces of a top treatment, often shaped like a tie, cone, cylinder or mini-cascade, which are generally used between and over swags as decoration and to hide seams.

Jamb: Interior side of a door or window frame.

Kerf: (kerfs, kerfing, kerfed) A channel created by a saw. These cuts are usually about 1/2 to 1 inch apart and halfway through the thickness of the board. This will allow the board to bend to desired shapes.

Kick pleat: An inverted pleat used at the corner of a cascade or return. The center of this pleat "kicks out" as it turns the corner and will hang to the effect of an additional pleat.

Lambrequin: A top treatment that is constructed on a wood frame, padded and covered with fabric. In some areas, a lambrequin only refers to such a top treatment with "legs" that extend to the floor: a cornice that completely frames the window.

L Bracket: (aka angle irons) A metal bracket in the shape of an L, used to install valance and cornices.

Leading edge: Opposite of return edge. The leading edges of a pair of pinch pleat draperies are the two edges that overlap. On stationary panels, they frame the glass.

Lengthwise grain: (aka warp) The threads in a woven fabric that run parallel to the selvages. Fabrics are stronger along the lengthwise grain.

Lining: A fabric that is used for the back of the window treatment. This fabric should be compatible with the face fabric.

Lip: The twill tape attached to ready-made twisted rope cord used as a seam allowance; or, refers to the seam allowance of a self-welt cord.

Long point: (aka deep point) The measurement of a treatment at its deepest area.

Master carrier: Two arms that overlap in the center of rod when draperies are closed, allowing draperies to overlap and close completely.

Memory stitch: (aka flagging) A stitch usually by hand done in the back of the drapery used to keep the lining and face in even folds.

Mending plates: A flat metal strip with holes for screws, used to join two pieces of lumber.

Micro cord: (aka Boston edge) 1.8 mm shade cord (normally used for stringing roman and balloon shades) that is covered with fabric and used in the same manner as standard fabric cord.

Millennium tape: A double-sided bonding tape made by 3M that is used by burnishing, or rubbing, it in. The longer this tape is on the fabric, the stronger the bond becomes.

Mitering: The joining of two surfaces evenly at an angle.

Mullion: The vertical wood or masonry sections between two window frames.

Multi-draw: A simultaneous opening and closing of several draperies on one rod at one time.

Muntin: The horizontal and vertical wood strips that separate panes of glass in windows.

Nominal Lumber: The actual measurement of stock boards differs from the nominal measurement. A 1 x 2 board is actually 3/4 inch x 1 1/2 inches, a 1 x 4 board is actually 3/4 inch x 3 1/2 inches, a 1 x 6 board is actually 3/4 inch x 5 1/2 inches and a 1 x 8 board is actually 3/4 inch x 7 1/4 inches. Be sure to measure the board for accuracy.

Off-center-draw: Draperies that traverse to a non-centered point.

One-way-draw: One panel of drapery designed to draw one way.

Opera draperies: Draperies that when raised, form scallops at the bottom, with the highest point in the middle and progressively lower scallops to each side forming an inside arch.

Outside measurement: Measurements taken of the outside perimeter of the window frame so that the treatment will cover all window facings.

Outside mount (OSM): The hardware for treatment is mounted on the outside of the window on the frame or wall and the treatment is not against any structure on the ends.

Overlap: The portion of fabric that overlaps (crosses over) in the middle of a pair of draperies when they are closed. When two swags cross over each other on a board or pole, that is the cross over or overlap area. The standard overlap for Kirsch and Graber traverse rods is 3 1/2 inches.

Pagoda cornice: A cornice with face and sides that flare outward and/or upward.

Pair width: Rod width plus one overlap and two returns. This is a measurement you would get if you took two panels of a pair of pinch pleat draperies and you laid them down end to end widthwise, not overlapping. When closed, the draperies should hug the traverse rod.

Panel: One-half of a pair of draperies or curtains, even though it may consist of several widths of fabric.

Panel width: The pair width divided by 2. This is the finished width of a panel of draperies.

Tassel trim is delicately sewn by hand onto a curtain panel border.

Passementerie: (aka Trims) The French term for a range of decorative cords, bands and tassels used on window fashions and furnishings, to give definition or add decorative detail.

Pattern repeat:(aka repeat) the distance between any given point in a design and where that exact point first appears again. Repeats can be horizontal or vertical.

Picture window: A type of window with a large center glass area with usually two smaller glass areas on each side.

Pillowcase: (aka pillowslip) The technique where face fabric and lining fabric are seamed together, usually with a 1/2-inch seam, then turned and pressed so the seam becomes the very edge of the item.

Pillowcase heading: The heading of a pinch pleat drapery is pillowcased with the buckram stitched in the seam and may have anywhere from 1/2-inch to 1-inch seam allowance.

Pin-on-hook: A metal pin to fasten draperies to a rod. It pins into the drapery pleat and hooks onto the traverse carrier, café rod or to a ring.

Pinch pleats: (aka French pleat) A drapery heading where the basic pleat is on the right side of the fabric and is divided into three smaller, equal folds sewn together at the bottom edge.

Piping: A term used in the apparel industry for cording.

Pleat: A fold of cloth sewn into place to create fullness.

Pleated balloon shade: A balloon shade made with box pleats.

Pleated roman shade: A roman shade with horizontal pleats, usually 4 inches to 8 inches deep, accented by stitching at the front and back of each crisp pleat; sometimes referred to as a Venetian (aka tucked) roman or a stitched roman.

Pleat to: A finished width of the fabric after it has been pleated.

Pleat to pleat: The measurement from the first pleat to the last pleat.

Pleater tape: Pocketed heading material designed to be used with slip in pleating hooks.

Pouf: The three dimensional informal scallop created by the way the treatment hangs, e.g., balloon valances and shades.

Pouf valance: A top treatment similar to the cloud, but the effect is one continuous pouf rather that separate poufs, and the pouf valance does not have a skirt.

Pressing: Lifting and lowering an iron set at an appropriate temperature in an overlapping pattern to avoid stretching fabric as ironing (sliding the iron up and down over the fabric) would.

Projection: (aka return) The distance from the front of the window treatment to the wall.

Proportion: The size relationship of one part of an object to other parts of the object.

Puddle: Formed by drapery panels, puddles are long enough to literally lie on the floor. Extra length must be added from 1 to 18 inches, depending upon the effect desired.

Pull: The knob on the end of the cords used to operate shades or draperies. It also refers to the side from which a shade is pulled, whether right pull or left pull.

PVC pole: A strong but lightweight plastic plumbing pipe. This can be found at plumbing supply and home improvement stores. Must be covered with fabric or painted.

Railroad: To turn fabric so the selvage runs across the treatment instead of up and down. 118-inch sheer is made to be used this way so that pinch pleats are put in across the selvage end instead of across the cut end. This can eliminate seams on some treatments.

Ready-mades: Standard size draperies, factory made and available at local stores or through mail order houses.

Repeat: See "Pattern repeat."

Return: The distance from the face of the rod to the wall or casing where the bracket or board is attached.

Reverse sham: An extra piece of fabric, attached to the head of a bedspread, which folds back over the pillows laying on the bedspread to cover them. Not meant to be tucked under pillows.

Rod pocket: A hollow sleeve in the top and sometimes in the bottom of a curtain or drapery through which a rod is inserted. The rod is then attached to the wall.

Roman Shade: (aka flat roman shade) A tailored fabric shade that hangs flat at the window; soft pleats form at the bottom as the shade is raised.

Roman valance: A soft, stationary valance fabricated similarly to a roman shade with stationary horizontal folds.

Rosette: A fabric accent constructed to resemble an open rose. It is often used to accessorize a window fashion or disguise an area of construction.

Ruched header: A method of gathering by incorporating extra fabric; this can be done by using shirring tape or adding extra fullness into rod pocket headers.

Running foot: (RF) The same as linear foot. A method of measuring by counting the length or width by the number of feet in the treatment.

Sash curtain: Any sheer material hung close to the window glass. Usually hung from spring tension rods or sash rods mounted inside the window casing.

Sash rod: A small rod, either decorative or plain.

Scab: A thin strip of fiberboard or lumber glued over a seam that joins two pieces of lumber.

Scale: Relationship between an object's size and the size of the space in which it is located.

Scalloped heading: A popular top treatment for café curtains featuring semi-circular spaces between pleats.

Self-lined: The face of the fabric is also used as the lining.

The Handy Jr. Button Machine has become increasingly popular as window treatments have become more elaborate and use buttons more often. The Button Machine works with a series of dies, button molds and wire eye backs, compressing the die together to form a covered button.

Selvedge: (aka selvage) The tightly woven edge on the length of the fabric to hold the fabric together.

Shade: An operational device used to reduce or screen light or heat.

Shade cord: Strong lift cord used to string through rings, screw eyes, pulleys and locks on roman, Austrian and balloon shades.

Shirred: Gathered.

Shirred roman shade: Fabric is shirred onto horizontal ribs and operates as a roman shade.

Shirring tapes: Heading material used to create pleats, gathers, smocking and other decorative headings.

Short point: The measurement a treatment will hang at its shortest area.

Side hem: The turned part forming a finished edge at the side of the drapery.

Single hem: The hem of the treatment has only 1/2 inch to 1 inch turned down inside to make a fold for sewing to the body fabric.

Single top: Heading in which the fabric is turned down the back and is finished either by turning 1/2 inch to 1 inch under the bottom of it or by serging the bottom along the edge of the buckram.

Sill: The horizontal "ledge-like" portion of a window casing.

Sleeve: A decorative casing made to cover a rod without a panel hanging below. It may or may not have a header or skirt.

Slides: (aka carriers) Small runners installed in a traverse rod, which hold a drapery pin or hook.

Slouch drapery panel: A type of drapery panel generally made without traditional pleats. It is a more casual style where the fabric along the heading is wavy to very loose, and the fabrication method for the heading can be any type depending on desired look. For example: pleats of any type, tabs, tucks or none at all, with or without buckram or crinoline.

Soft cornice: A flat stiffened fabric valance attached to a mount board with or without legs.

Spacing: Refers to the flat space between the pleats.

Stack back: (aka stack up) The amount of space taken up by a drapery or shade when they are completely open.

Stacking: The area required for draperies when they are completely opened.

Stationary panels: Purely decorative drapery panels that do not open or close.

Stay stitch: A row of long stitching, just inside the seam line, to prevent stretching and to protect the grain line.

Sunburst: A semicircular window fashion used in arch-top windows or above rectangular windows to give the appearance of an arch-top window. Fabric is shirred around the circumference of the circle and gathered at the lower center.

Swag: A fabric top treatment that drapes into soft semicircular folds of fabric. Swags can be used with draperies or as a top treatment only.

Swing arm: A hinged metal curtain rod that swings away to uncover a window fully.

Tabling: Measuring a treatment and marking it to the finished length before the final finishing.

Tack strip:

A. Window treatments: A piece of fabric attached to a valance at the top to finish the raw edges and to allow for it to be mounted on the board.

B. Upholstery: A thin, cardboard strip, 3/8 inch or 1/2 inch wide, used to prevent fabric from puckering between staples and to give a sharp, even edge.

Tieback: A decorative element used to gather drapery panels to the center or sides of a window opening to allow light and ventilation. It is also for aesthetic purposes as part of the design process.

Top treatment: Any decorative design at the top of a window. Top treatments can either stand-alone or be incorporated as part of a larger window treatment design. Includes cornices, valances, swags, etc.

Total width: The width of the board or rod, end to end, plus two returns.

Traverse: To draw across. A traverse drapery is one that opens and closes across a window by means of the traverse rod from which it is hung.

T-Square: An instrument consisting of two pieces used for testing the accuracy of square work and for making right angles.

Tuft: Clusters of thread drawn tightly through a pillow or cushion or furniture that holds the fabric and padding in place.

Turn of cloth: The minute ease of fabric that is lost from making a fold.

Twill tape: A strong (sew on) tape that has a diagonal weave.

Under-draperies: A lightweight drapery, usually a sheer, closest to the window glass. It hangs beneath a heavier over-draper.

Upson board: A type of fiberboard that is made from 100 percent recycled components. Sometimes used to construct cornice boards. It is lightweight and comes in 1/4-inch and 3/8-inch thickness and is easy to work with.

Valance: A horizontal decorative fabric treatment used at the top of draperies to screen hardware and cords or as a stand-alone decorative element.

Valance board: (aka mount board or dust board) The flat board without a front or sides from which a valance is hung.

Valance board with legs: A flat board with boards extending down each return end. It looks like a cornice without the front. This board is used when it is necessary to anchor the sides of the valance.

Waste: Any fabric that is leftover or not used in the finished produce, e.g., excess parts of the repeats.

Weights, chain and lead: Lead weights are sewn in at the vertical seams and each corner of drapery panel. Chain weights are small heavy beads strung in a line along bottom hemline of sheers, to ensure an even hemline and straight hanging.

Welting: See "Cording."

Width: A word to describe a single width of fabric (from selvage to selvage). Several widths of fabric are sewn together to make a panel of drapery.

Wiggle Board: See "Bendable lauan."

Window jewelry: Small pieces of decorative hardware used as accents on fabric, usually serving no functional purpose but to add interest.

Resource Guide

Hardware

Alamo Heights Ironworks
PO Box 6563
San Antonio, TX 78209-6563
Telephone: (866) 820-3555, (210) 820-3555
Fax: (210) 820-3555
Website: http://alamoheightsironworks.com
To the trade only
Custom designed and fabricated drapery and tapestry hardware, wrought-iron valances, wall plaques, fireplace screens, pot racks and other home accessories

Alhambra Hardware Co., Inc.
90 Tycos Dr.
Toronto, ON M6B 1V9
Telephone: (800) 461-0060, (426) 780-1707
Fax: (416) 780-1814
Website: www.alhambra-hardware.com
E-mail: info@steptoewife.com
Available through designers and specialty retailers
Extensive collection of drapery hardware, finials and accessories; design and manufacture Curtains UpTM

Amore Drapery Hardware
12121 Veteran's Memorial Dr., Ste. 2
Houston, TX 77067
Telephone: (281) 440-0123
Fax: (281) 440-0214
Website: www.amoredraperyhardware.com
Available through local designers and dealers
Extensive line of decorative metal drapery hardware and fittings

Artizan Wood Drapery Hardware
10022 NW 46th St.
Sunrise, FL 33351
Telephone: (800) 448-7932
Fax: (954) 749-0606
Website: www.woodrods.com
E-mail: Mike@WoodRods.com
To the trade only
Specializing in the manufacturing of elegant wood drapery hardware and decorative finials; also in custom bow and bay window drapery rods

Bentley Brothers
2709 S Park Rd.
Louisville, KY 40219
Telephone: (800) 824-4777
Fax: (502) 969-1702
Website: www.bentleybrothers.com
Available through local distributors
Extensive line of decorative drapery hardware in Arts and Crafts styles; also wood, forged iron and cast resin

FancyWindows.Com
6 Bitterwood Cir.
The Woodlands, TX 77381
Telephone: (281) 380-4790—please call between 6PM & 10PM central time
Fax: (626) 608-3649
Website: www.fancywindows.com
E-mail: info@fancywindows.com
Custom window treatment hardware

Golden Finial Collection, Inc.
1744 Norman St. #1
Ridgewood, NY 11385
Telephone: (718) 366-1863
Fax: (718) 366-3688
Website: www.goldenfinial.com
E-mail: sales@goldenfinial.com
Sales to business accounts only
Highest quality decorative drapery hardware

J. L. Anthony Custom Drapery Hardware
(a division of Lancaster & Associates, Inc.)
Dallas, TX 75238
Telephone: (214) 340-0359
Fax: (214) 340-3108
Website: www.jlanthony.com
E-mail: info@jlanthony.com
To the trade only
Distinctive drapery hardware

K-Blair Finials
2870 N Berkeley Lake Rd., Ste. 3
Duluth, GA 30096
Telephone: (770) 622-1972
Fax: (770) 622-1975
Website: www.k-blairfinials.com
E-mail: kay@k-blairfinials.com
To the trade only
Custom drapery rods and hardware, hand-cut crystal finials, medallions, swag-holders, holdbacks

Kirsch
Telephone: (800) 538-6567
Website: www.kirsch.com
E-mail: info@kirsch.com
Dealers nationwide
Decorative drapery hardware

M & T Drapes
Telephone: (800) 715-1008, (970) 240-8494
Fax: (347) 412-7237
Website: www.mtdrapes.com
E-mail: mtdrapes@mtdrapes.com
Direct consumer sales
Comprehensive collection of curtain and drapery hardware, plus related items. Lines carried include Kirsch, Graber, Kaleidoscope, wrought iron, hand-

carved wood components, cast resin finials and Century Architectural Specialties

Orion Ornamental Iron, Inc.
6918 Tujunga Ave.
North Hollywood, CA 91605
Telephone: (877) 476-6278
Website: www.ironartbyorion.com
Wholesale trade only
Design and manufacture of decorative drapery hardware

Paso Robles Ironworks
1236 Railroad St.
Paso Robles, CA 93446
Telephone: (800) 549-9754
Website: www.ironhardware.com
E-mail: ironhardware@sbcglobal.net
Elegant iron curtain rods, hand-forged hardware, lighting

Phillips Metal Works
313 E Jefferson St.
Montgomery, AL 36104
Telephone: (334) 263-9931
Fax: (334) 263-9931
Website: www.phillipsmetalworks.com
E-mail: john@phillipsmetalworks.com
Contemporary wrought-iron drapery rods, finials, lighting, furniture

Premier Windowwear
255 Ottley Dr. NE
Atlanta, GA 30324-3926
Telephone: (800) 251-5800, (404) 873-6000
Fax: (800) 251-2515, (404) 873-9993
Website: www. premierwindowwear.com
E-mail: info@premierwindowwear.com
Wholesale resource for artistic drapery hardware and ornamental accessories; no white goods, fabric, trimmings or blinds

Skotz Manufacturing
Telephone: (800) 624-6763
Website: www.magnerod.com
Wholesale to the trade, available at retailers nationwide
The Original MagneRod, the new self-adhesive Miracle Rod and other fine window hardware
Headquartered in Philadelphia

Susan Goldstick Incorporated
465 Coloma St., Ste. A
Sausalito, CA 94965-2871
Telephone: (415) 332-6719
Website: www.susangoldstick.com
Elaborate drapery finials, tiebacks, rods, brackets, window accessories, knobs and furniture

21st Century Drapery Hardware, Inc.
52 Meadow Ln.
New Hope, PA 18938
Telephone: (215) 862-2209
Fax: (215) 862-9215
Website: www.finials.com
E-mail: finials21@aol.com
Featuring an extraordinary line of distinctive maple wood hardware

Unsworth and Avers
Sales and marketing:
302 S Payne St.
Alexandria, VA 22314
Telephone: (703) 684-6526
Fax: (703) 684-6526
Production and distribution:
3074 Pacific Ave.
San Francisco, CA 94115
Telephone: (415) 928-4895
Fax: (415) 928-4895
Website: www.unsworthandavers.com
E-mail: info@unsworthandavers.com
Elegant, high quality decorative drapery hardware and accessories, including new bamboo line

Vesta
Telephone: (800) 638-3782
Website: www.ivesta.com
To the trade only
Exquisite drapery hardware

Worldwide Window Treatments LLC/
Gould Drapery Hardware
840 Barry St.
Bronx, NY 10474
Telephone: (800) 223-8990, (718) 893-9370
Fax: (718) 893-4788
Website: www.wwtgould.com
E-mail: wwtgould@aol.com
Decorative and functional wood and metal drapery hardware

Fabric/Trim

Brimar
28250 Ballard Dr.
Lake Forest, IL 60045-4536
Telephone: (847) 247-0100
Website: www.brimarinc.com
Carried by dealers nationwide
Brimar offers the finest quality selection of tassels, tiebacks, trimmings and drapery hardware

Clarence House
979 Third Ave., Ste. 205
New York, NY 10022
Telephone: (800) 221-4704, (800) 632-0076,
(212) 752-2890
Fax: (212) 755-3314
Website: www.clarencehouse.com

To the trade only; products available exclusively through interior decorators, architects and designers. Hand screen-printed fabrics and wallpapers, hand-loomed brocades, also the highest-quality velvets, damasks, silks, cottons, linens, sheers, trimmings and leathers

I Luv Fabrix
3938 Chesswood Dr.
North York, ON M3J 2W6
Telephone: (416) 398-7584
Website: www.iluvfabrix.com
E-mail: info@iluvfabrix.com
Featuring fabrics by Scalamandré, Clarence House, Colfax and Fowler, Brunschwig; design service by Michelle Tennen

Scalamandré
Scalamandré Showroom:
222 E 59th St. Suites 110/210/310
New York, NY 10022
Telephone: (212) 980-3888
Fax: (212) 688-7531
Website: www.scalamandre.com
Email: nyshowroom@scalamandre.com,
info@scalamandre.com
To the trade only
America's manufacturer and importer of the world's most beautiful fabrics, trimmings, wallcoverings and carpets

Trimland
USA office:
60 E Jefryn Blvd.
Deer Park, NY 11729
Telephone: (631) 667-2333, (877) TRIMLAND
Fax: (631) 667-0033
Website: www.trimland.com
E-mail: USA@trimland.com
To the trade; international retailers
High end trimmings for curtains and upholstery

Specialties

Alameda Shade Shop
914 Central Ave.
Alameda, CA 94501
Telephone: (510) 522-0633
Fax: (510) 522-0651
Website: www.shadeshop.com
Elegant Victorian roller shades, extensive materials and trim selection

Amazon Dry Goods
411 Brady St.
Davenport, IA 52801
Telephone: (800) 798-7979
Fax: (563) 322-4003
Website: www.amazondrygoods.com
E-mail: info@amazondrygoods.com
Period window treatment patterns; other period items

Ann Wallace & Friends
PO Box 2344
Venice, CA 90294
Telephone: (213) 614-1757
Fax: (213) 614-1758
Website: www.annwallace.com
E-mail: wallgab@earthlink.net
Custom curtains for Arts and Crafts homes, variety of fabrics and details; period-appropriate curtain hardware

Archive Edition Textiles
12575 Crenshaw Blvd.
Hawthorne, CA 90250
Telephone: (877) 676-2424, (310) 676-2424
Fax: (310) 676-2424
Website: www.archiveedition.com
E-mail: textileguy@aol.com
Custom draperies or window treatments; authentic Arts and Crafts styles and true period colors

Arts & Crafts Period Textiles
5427 Telegraph Ave.
Oakland, CA 94609
Telephone: (510) 654-1645
Website: www.textilestudio.com
E-mail: ACPTextile@aol.com
Hand-embroidered, appliquéd and stenciled curtains; fabric, embroidery kits and curtain hardware

Eaton Hill Textile Works
334 Jake Martin Rd.
Marshfield, VT 05658
Telephone: (802) 426-3733
Website: www.eatonhilltextiles.com
E-mail: kateehtw@aol.com
Reproduced 18th- and 19th-century historic textiles for window treatments, upholstery, carpeting and bedding

Glyders
Vavco LLC
Lake Havasu City, AZ 86406
Telephone: (928) 505-1070
Website: www.glyders.com
Unique door and window treatments, made with hardwoods and natural fabrics—ideal for sliding doors or windows, room dividers and privacy screens

The Handwerk Shade Shop
PO Box 22455
Portland, OR 97222
Telephone: (503) 659-0914
Website: www.thehandwerkshop.com
Custom crafted roller shades; hand-stenciled permanent designs on these custom shades is also available

Indian Creek Interiors / Indian Creek
Design Studio
115 W 2nd St.
Shamrock, TX 79079
Telephone: (806) 256-2707
Fax: (806) 256-2707
Website: www.indiancreekleather.com
E-mail: go@indiancreekleather.com
Retail and wholesale custom leather window treatments and accessories
Gaylynn Otts, Owner and Designer

John E. Hinkel, Inc.
1680 Williams Rd.
PO Box 865
Monroe, NC 28111
Telephone: (800) 348-2780, (704) 283-5919
Fax: (704) 282-0088
Website: www.johnehinkel.com
E-mail: info@johnehinkel.com
Commercial window coverings
Extensive custom window treatments, including motorized systems and flame retardant fabrics; also manufactures custom designed valances of all types

J. R. Burrows & Co.
PO Box 522
Rockland, MA 2370
Telephone: (800) 347-1795, (781) 982-1812
Fax: (781) 982-1636
Website: www.burrows.com
E-mail: merchant@burrows.com
Scottish lace curtains; also classic Arts and Crafts furnishings

London Lace
89 W Concord St.
Boston, MA 02118
Telephone: (800) 926-LACE, (617) 267-3506
Website: www.londonlace.com
E-mail: sales@londonlace.com
Finest Scottish lace window treatments created on the original Victorian looms using vintage patterns, plus more contemporary designs; antique lines from Scotland available in-store only

Quality Cornices
7081 S Eudora St.
Centennial, CO 80122
Telephone: (303) 850-7010
Fax: (303) 850-7010
Website: www.qualitycornices.com
E-mail: brevell@qwest.net
Custom cornice boards, lambrequins, folding screens, headboards and mirror frame

CUSTOM AND READY-MADE PRODUCTS

Abbey Window Coverings
5440 Hollybridge Way
Richmond, BC V7C 4N3
Telephone: (800) 663-1606, (604) 279-0021
Fax: (604) 279-0885
Website: www.abbeywindowcoverings.com
Authorized dealers throughout Canada
Wholesale manufacturer and distributor of custom window coverings

Artisan Interiors
Corporate Office
526 South Main St.
Middlebury, IN 46540
Telephone: (219) 825-9494
Artisan Longmont Office
455 Weaver Park Rd.
Longmont, CO 80501
Telephone: (800) 344-7384
Website: www.artisan-interiors.com
E-mail: info@artisan-interiors.com
Drapery hardware, custom window treatments

BlindsandDrapery.com, L.L.C.
10000 W 75th St.
Hodgkins, IL 60525
Telephone: (800) 630-3007
Fax: (800) 630-6306
Website: www.blindsanddrapery.com
Comprehensive array of window treatments at discount prices, bedding and accessories also

Calico Corners
Telephone: (800) 213-6366
Website: www.calicocorners.com
Window treatments, fabrics, bedding, furniture, more; design associates available
Stores nationwide

Cincinnati Window Décor
3004 Harris Ave.
Cincinnati, OH 45212
Telephone: (800) 853-6214, (513) 631-7200
Fax: (513) 631-8882
Website: www.cincishade.com
E-mail: cshade@cinti.net
Featuring Kirsch, Graber, Hunter Douglas and Levolor products; also specialty items

Claire Fabrics
Website: www.clairefabrics.com
E-mail: claire@clairefabrics.com
Sold through local dealers
Decorative drapery rods, fabrics, custom window treatments

Curtain Calls
181 Bluffton Hwy. Ste. B104
Magnolia Village, Bluffton, SC 29910
Telephone: (843) 815-2371
Website: www.curtaincallsco.com
E-mail: Karen@curtaincallsco.com
Shutters, blinds, draperies, window top treatments, soft shades, bedding, furniture and lighting
Authorized dealer for DrapeStyle

Curzon USA
680 8th St., Ste. 166
San Francisco, CA 94103
Telephone: (415) 626-9038
Fax: (415) 626-9038
E-mail: inform@curzon.co.za;
curzon_usa@hotmail.com
Website: www.curzon.co.za
In Canada:
Decor Accents
310 Davenport Rd., Ste. 202
Toronto, ON M5R 1K6
Telephone: (416) 977-9967
Fax: (416) 977-8110
Website: www.curzon.co.za
E-mail: info@decoraaccents.com
Available through dealers nationwide
Custom draperies, full line of window treatment hardware, finials; also interior lighting and fixtures, mirror frames, decorative ornaments and furniture

Decorating Den Interiors
National Headquarters:
8659 Commerce Dr.
Easton, MD 21601
Telephone: (800) dec-dens
Website: www.decoratingden.com
Decorators are located throughout the United States, Canada and United Kingdom and offer convenient, in-home consultations on design, including drapery, wall covering, flooring, furniture and accessories.

Denver Fabrics / Denverfabrics.com
Main Store & Annex South:
2777 W. Belleview
Littleton, CO 80123-2953
Telephone: (303) 730-2777
Website: www.denverfabrics.com
Featuring Houlés decorative drapery hardware, fabrics, drapery construction supplies

DrapeStyle
Telephone: (877) 814-6760
Website: www.drapestyle.com
E-mail: inquiries@drapestyle.com
(Curtain Calls is also a DrapeStyle dealer: www.curtaincallsco.com)
Just drapes: finest quality silk and linen drapery at the very best price available

Expression Décor
193 E Altadena Dr.
Altadena, CA 91001
Telephone: (626) 445-1135, (800) 439-5255
Website: www.expressiondecor.com
E-mail: expressiond@earthlink.net
Elegant to very elaborate custom window treatments; also custom bedding, furniture, home accessories

Gamache & Lessard
995 Center St.
Auburn, ME 04210
Telephone: (207) 782-0052
Website: www.gamachelessard.com
Quality custom roller shades; wide variety of other window treatments available

Hunter Douglas
2 Pkwy & Rt. 17 South
Upper Saddle River, NJ 07458
Telephone: (800) 937-STYLE
Website: www.hunterdouglas.com
Available through dealers worldwide
Leading manufacturer of the widest selection of custom window fashions

Interior Décor, Inc.
5650 Tomken Rd., Units 1 & 2
Mississauga, ON L4W 4P1
Telephone: (866) 217-7779, (905) 501-7779
Fax: (905) 507-9777
Website: www.einteriordecor.com
E-mail: info@einteriordecor.com
Full line of custom window treatments; also bedding and fabrics by the yard

InteriorMall.com
1004 22nd St.
Barling, AK 72923
Telephone: (800) 590-5844, (479) 452-3025
Fax: (479) 452-3092
Website: www.interiormall.com
Highest quality custom window treatments at discounted prices; other interior decorating services

Smith + Noble
Telephone: (800) 560-0027
Website: www.smithandnoble.com
E-mail: contactus@smithnoble.com
Custom window treatments and home décor

DESIGNERS

A Personal Touch
5622 Willow Valley Rd.
Clifton, VA 20124-0962
Telephone: (703) 968-8901
Fax: (703) 968-8901
E-mail: sewtiger@earthlink.net
Karen Moy

Accent Draperys, Inc.
1515 Chamberlayne Ave.
Richmond, VA 23222
Telephone: (804) 329-3930
Fax: (804) 329-3932
E-mail: accentdraperys@comcast.net
Window treatment designer, workroom
Karen Hardy

ADM Interiors
88 Forestburgh Rd.
Monticello, NY 12701
Telephone: (845) 794-7900
Fax: (845) 794-7920
E-mail: adm88@verizon.net
Window treatment designer, installer, workroom
Nella Velasco

Alexis Ulrich Interior Design
PO Box 305
Los Gatos, CA 95031-0305
Telephone: (408) 369-1506
Fax: (408) 369-8406
Window treatments, other interior design

ALS Interiors
884 Spruce Cir.
Harleysville, PA 19438
Telephone: (215) 256-1712
Fax: (215) 256-1712
E-mail: Sharayko@enter.net
Window treatments, other interior design
April Sharayko, WFCP, CID

Ann Cogburn Custom Draperies
5701 Murphy Rd.
Sachse, TX 75048
Telephone: (972) 495-7779
Cell: (972) 679-0547
Fax: (972) 495-5394
Website: www.custom-draperies.com
E-mail: ann@cogburn.net
Custom draperies and window treatments; also custom furniture and upholstery

Anna Rodé Designs
17005 Castello Cir.
San Diego, CA 92127
Telephone: (858) 759-2662
Cell: (858) 414-1009
Fax: (858) 759-2665
Website: www.annarodedesigns.com
Window treatments, interior design for fine Southern California homes and businesses
Coleen Choisser, IIDA, CCIDC

Annalisa Designs
1188 Queen Ln. Apt. #4
West Chester, PA 19382
Telephone: (484) 905-5306
E-mail: atorrente@endlesspools.com
Window treatment designer/decorator
Annalisa Torrente

Angela's Custom Interiors
12967 Stanford Dr.
Victorville, CA 92392
Telephone: (760) 241-8564
Fax: (760) 241-2885
E-mail: angelasinteriors@msn.com
Interior designer specializing in custom window fashions
Angela Zerkich

Arlington Crest Design Studio
1867 N Adams St.
Arlington, VA 22201
Telephone: (703) 524-3679
Fax: (703) 524-0080
E-mail: r.schweigert@verizon.net
Window treatment designer, installer, workroom
Rick A. Schweigert, Prop. CWP CWTC

Beale-Lana Interior Design
300 E 57th St.
New York, NY 10022
Telephone: (212) 813-2213
Website: www.beale-lana.com
E-mail: info@beale-lana.com
B. Randall Beale and Carl Lana

Bennett and Judie Weinstock Interiors
The Barclay 4B
237 S Eighteenth St.
Philadelphia, PA 19103
Telephone: (215) 735-2026

Blue Ribbon Interiors
15 Mayhew Rd.
Attleboro, MA 02703-1601
Telephone: (508) 223-1400
Fax: (508) 223-2299
E-mail: kfredrickson@earthlink.net
Kelly B.

Cabin to Castle Interior Design Services
2 Summit Dr.
Lake George, NY 12845
Telephone: (518) 668-0188, (518) 668-3866
Website: www.cabintocastleinteriors.com
E-mail: Doris@CabinToCastleInteriors.com
Fine custom window treatments, dealer for Hunter Douglas window products; other interior design services

Canterberri Designs
7 Avery Ln.
Sterling, MA 01564-2238
Telephone: (978) 422-8766
E-mail: cberridesigns@comcast.net
Custom Drapery Workroom
Kymberlee Odoardi

Carlette Cormier
131 White Magnolia Cir.
Savannah, GA 31419
Telephone: (912) 920-7802

Charlotte's Custom Draperies & Home Fashions
327 Garner Run Rd.
Waynesburg, PA 15370
Telephone: (724) 627-9320
Fax: (724) 627-3578
E-mail: ccsews@alltel.net
Charlotte Connors, CWP

Christina Miller Interiors
26096 Avenida Bonachon
Mission Viejo, CA 92691
Telephone: (949) 597-9211
Fax: (949) 597-9211

Christine Cavallaro Designs
5 Nicoll Dr.
Andover, MA 01810-6052
Telephone: (978) 470-2578
E-mail: cavallarodesigns@comcast.net
Window treatment designer, installer, workroom
Christine Cavallaro, CWP CWTC

Classic Touch Design
143 Inverness Dr.
Blue Bell, PA 19422
Telephone: (610) 313-9008
Fax: (610) 313-9008
E-mail: classictouchdesign@comcast.net
Designer window treatments and decorative accessories
LeeAnn Reed, CWP

Classy Shades
351 Snug Harbor Dr.
Lopez Island, WA 98261
Telephone: (360) 468-3329
E-mail: kathy@classyshades.com
Custom fabric shades and bedding decor
Katherine Cade, CWTC

The Cornice Board
10 Truman Dr.
Farmingville, NY 11738
Telephone: (631) 732-8291
Fax: (631) 732-8291
E-mail: cornice@optonline.net
Interior Decorator and Designer
Lynne Turnquist and Mary Ann Schultz, CWP, CWTC

Creations by Corrine, L.L.C.
1221 Streaker Rd.
Sykesville, MD 21784
Telephone: (410) 795-3506
Fax: (410) 795-3889
E-mail: corrine_z@hotmail.com
Window treatment designer, installer, workroom
Corrine Zwiselsberger, CWTC

Creative Influence
2327 Young Rd.
Stone Mountain, GA 30088
Telephone: (770) 322-9343
E-mail: GINGERS900@MSN.COM
Creative window treatments and upholstery design
Virginia Thompson

Crystal Mowery, Design Consultant
Calico Corners
4004 Hillsboro Rd.
Nashville, TN 37215
Telephone: (615) 269-4551

Curtain Call
1225 3rd Ave.
Gilbertsville, PA 19525
Telephone: (610) 406-1493
Fax: (610) 906-1140
E-mail: curtaincallforu@comcast.net
Window treatment designer, installer, workroom
Susan Forbes

Custom Interior Creations
16310 Goshen Rd.
Montpelier, VA 23192
Telephone: (804) 883-7299
Fax: (804) 883-7299

Custom Window Decor
926 Ozone Ave.
Santa Monica, CA 90405-5702
Telephone: (310) 396-5822
Fax: (310) 396-5314
E-mail: customwindowdecor@earthlink.net
Window treatment designer, installer, workroom
Conrad M. Melilli, CWP CWTC

Custom Window Products, Inc.
11 Grand View Ave.
Mattapoisett, MA 02739-2334
Telephone: (508) 758-3122
Fax: (508) 355-8791
E-mail: customwindowpro@comcast.net
Ginny Rivenburg, CWTC

Danziger Design
30 Matthew Cir.
Richboro, PA 18954
Telephone: (215) 322-5666
Fax: (215) 322-4202
E-mail: danzigerdesign@hotmail.com
Window treatment designer
Adele Danziger

Decor Elan
119 W Main St.
Salisbury, MD 21801
Telephone: (443) 783-4978
Fax: (410) 749-0703
E-mail: jenny@decorelan.com
Full-service interior design, custom window treatments and other soft furnishings, custom closet solutions, unique furnishings, accessories, and bedding options
Jennifer Payne

Decorating by Lisa.com
Bridgemill area, Canton, GA
Telephone: (678) 478-0504
Website: www.decoratingbylisa.com
Designing and sewing high quality, custom draperies for your home or office; free consultation

Decorating 101
57 Saratoga Ln.
Harleysville, PA 19438
Telephone: (215) 368-2599
E-mail: lynn@decorating101pa.com
Window treatment designer, installer, workroom
Lynn Faughey, CWP CWTC

Decorating with Fabric
442 Saddle River Rd.
Monsey, NY 10952
Telephone: (845) 352-5064
E-mail: neil@decoratingwithfabric.com
Neil Gordon

Designer's Image
Design Studio: Walled Lake, MI 48390
Telephone: (866) 424-1285
Fax: (248) 960-4478
Website: www.designersimage.net
E-mail: debbie@designersimage.net
Custom drapery and interiors; design consultation available to metro Detroit area; also special pricing for Hunter Douglas Blinds when ordered over the web

DeSigns by Clarice
Scottsdale, AZ 85251-1132
Telephone: (480) 941-0428
Fax: (480) 941-0428
Website: www.designsbyclarice.com
E-mail: designsbyclarice@prodigy.net
Full-service residential and contract interior design services

Designs By Mara, Inc.
6710 220th St. SW #2
Mountlake Terrace, WA 98043
Telephone: (425) 776-8265
Fax: (425) 776-5355
E-mail: dbm4art@comcast.net
Soft furnishings designer workroom
Mara Vollbrecht, CWP CWTC

Distinctive Decor Ltd.
3208 Rolling Green Dr.
Churchville, MD 21028-1312
Telephone: (410) 399-4440
Fax: (410) 734-6729

DM Designs
18 Long Boat Rd.
Bourne, MA 02532-2218
Telephone: (508) 888-7603
Fax: (508) 888-7603
Window treatments, other interior design work

Donna Elle Interior Design
9 Nobska Wy.
Nantucket, MA 02210
Telephone: (508) 228-4561
Fax: (508) 228-9781
Website: www.donnaelle.com
E-mail: donna@donnaelle.com
Donna Elle

Elizabeth-Kent Interiors
PO Box 1114
Brentwood, TN 37024
Telephone: (615) 661-0301
Beth Rhora

Embellishments
Telephone: (847) 441-8020
Website: http://winnetkainteriordesign.com
*A full service interior design studio located near
Chicago. By appointment*
Colleen Larkey

Ethan Allen
101 Cleveland Ave., Ste. 100
Bay Shore, NY 11706
Telephone: (631) 243-5243
Fax: (631) 243-3497
E-mail: roberta@restful-ea.com
Roberta Levine

Exclusive Draperies & Upholstery
14740 A Flint Lee Rd.
Chantilly, VA 20151
Telephone: (703) 968-9506
Fax: (703) 968-7681
E-mail: mtrunnell@edaui.com
Full service custom draperies
Matt Trunnell, CWP CWTC

Final Touch Design
35 Jackson Ave.
Syosset, NY 11791
Telephone: (516) 921-6228
Fax: (516) 921-6229
E-mail: darcydesign@aol.com
Full service design firm specializing in custom furnishings

Fine Designs
9 Gertz Ct.
Sacramento, CA 95823
Telephone: (916) 505-3439
Fax: (916) 244-0411
E-mail: info@finedesignsbydottie.com
Window treatment designer, workroom
Dottie Matheson, CWTC

First Impressions
117 Cruickshank Dr.
Folsom, CA 95630
Telephone: (916) 817-8748
Fax: (916) 817-4230
E-mail: c.pursle@sbcglobal.net
Window treatment designer, installer, workroom
Clara Pursley

The French Twist
461 Main St.
East Greenwich, RI 02818
Telephone: (401) 886-4666
Donna Morris

Gail Prauss Interior Design, Ltd.
421 N Marion St.
Oak Park, IL 60302
Telephone: (708) 524-1233
Fax: (708) 524-1237
Website: www.praussinteriors.com
E-mail: gpid@sbcglobal.net
*A full service design firm utilizing high quality
products, furnishings, and fabrications*

Georgina Rice & Co., Inc.
550 - 15th St., 3rd Floor
San Francisco, CA 94103
Telephone: (415) 241-7100
Fax: (415) 241-7101
E-mail: georgina@georginarice.com
Interior designer and workroom
Georgina Rice

HD Interiors
97 Saddle Hill Rd.
Hopkinton, MA 01748
Telephone: (508) 435-6794
Fax: (508) 435-9087
E-mail: sewdeco1@aol.com
Kathleen Faletra, CWP CWTC

Interior Concepts
PO Box 1617
Hockessin, DE 19707
Telephone: (302) 239-7770
Fax: (302) 239-7061

Jacobs' Upholstery, Inc. Interior Design Studio
16023 E Sprague Ave.
Spokane, WA 99037
Telephone: (800) 481-6033, (509) 926-4230
Fax: (509) 924-3916
Website: www.jacobsupholstery.com
Custom window treatments, bedding, upholstery

Jamie Gibbs & Associates
122 E 82nd St.
New York, NY 10028
Telephone: (212) 717-6590
Fax: (212) 369-6332
E-mail: jamiegibbsassocs@aol.com
Jamie Gibbs

JDS Designs, Inc.
528 Eighth St. NE
Washington, D.C. 20002
Telephone: (202) 543-8631
E-mail: devojds@aol.com
David Herchik and Richard Loomis

Jennifer Ferber Interiors
1 Lafayette Ct.
Poughkeepsie, NY 12603
Telephone: (845) 485-1992
Fax: (845) 485-1992
E-mail: jenferber@aol.com
Window treatment designer, workroom
Jennifer White

JLW Interiors
9900 Peach St.
Waterford, PA 16441
Telephone: (814) 796-6597
Fax: (814) 796-6597

John Rolland Interiors
The Barclay 4A
237 S Eighteenth St.
Philadelphia, PA 19103
Telephone: (215) 546-3223

Juliana's Home Interiors
13412 Cavalier Woods Dr.
Clifton, VA, 20124
Telephone: (866) 585-4262, (703) 266-6744
Fax: (703) 266-6743
Website: www.jhidesign.com
*Custom draperies and top treatments, bedding, fabrics,
other interior design services*

Katydid Custom Designs
7442 Van Noy Loop
Ft. Meade, MD 20755
Telephone: (410) 674-4728
E-mail: nuge5@comcast.net
Kathryn Nugent, CWTC

Kent Kiesey Interior Design
431 W Oakdale Ave.
Chicago, IL 60657
Telephone: (773) 528-9301

L.P. Carpenter Interiors
296 Main St.
Cohasset, MA 02025-2013
Telephone: (781) 383-2225
Dorothy Adams

Lesley Petty
1419 S Jackson, Studio 112
Seattle, WA 98144
Telephone: (206) 325-2622
E-mail: lesley@lesleypetty.com;
Window Treatments Workroom

Luxe Interiors
1021 Chestnut Glen
Athens, GA 30606-7648
Telephone: (706) 248-7062
E-mail: butlerdesign@bellsouth.net
*Design, creation, and installation of custom window
treatments of all kinds*
Kristina Butler

Magnolia Design Studios
Telephone: (301) 370-0115
E-mail:
magnoliadesignstudios@comcast.net
Felicia Zannino-Baker

Margaret Davidson
19203 Dry Slough Rd.
Mount Vernon, WA 98273-9555
Telephone: (360) 445-2605
E-mail: margar@cnw.com
Artist

Marilyn Warner
14104 Tern Dr.
Colorado Springs, CO 80921
Telephone: (719) 200-2297
E-mail: Austintru@aol.com
Austin Warner Interiors

Mariya Interior Decor
2709 E Commercial Blvd.
Fort Lauderdale, FL 33308
Telephone: (954) 772-3271
Fax: (954) 772-9246
Website: www.mariyainteriordecor.com
*High quality custom made window treatments, bedding,
soft and wood cornices, table skirts, cushions, decorative
pillows, slipcovers and a variety of other products.*
Designer: Mariya Orlovsky

Marc Tash Interiors
Serving all Boros, Westchester, lower CT,
Long Island and NJ
Telephone: (212) 385-2253, (718) 336-3326
Website: www.marctashinteriors.com
E-mail: marctash@worldnet.att.net
*An outstanding collection of unique window treatment
designs and window covering styles suitable for any
home décor*

Mark Garrett
666 Post St. # 701
San Francisco, CA. 94109
Telephone: (415) 674-6912

Mary Sherwood Lake Living, Inc.
326 Lizard Creek Rd.
Littleton, NC 27850
Telephone: (252) 586-2437
Fax: (252) 586-6599
Website: www.marysherwood.com
E-mail: info@marysherwood.com
*Window treatments, plus full range of interior
design services*

Mary's Custom Workroom
1261 Liberty Way, Ste. B
Vista, CA 92081
Telephone: (760) 734-3791
Fax: (760) 734-3799
E-mail: warnekefam@cox.net
Window treatment designer, installer, workroom
Mary Warneke, CWP CWTC

Material Things, Inc.
552 Rock Shadow Ct.
Stone Mountain, GA 30087
Telephone: (770) 413-2971
Fax: (770) 413-2971
E-mail: dovieinteriors@yahoo.com
*Design, fabricate and install custom window treat-
ments and soft furnishings*

Dovlane Ferguson, CWP
Meredith Moriarty
914 Harding Rd.
Hinsdale, IL 60521
Telephone: (630) 654-1879
E-mail: PSJM2MKM@aol.com

Nancy Stracka Interiors, Inc.
50 Londonderry Rd.
Marblehead, MA 01945
Telephone: (781) 639-0792
Fax: (781) 639-3268
Website: www.strackainteriors.com
Complete interior design services

Nancy Sutton Interior Design
2250 E Victory Dr., Ste. 103
Savannah, GA 31404
Telephone: (912) 356-9912

Not Just Curtains
11 Shipley Dr.
Cortlandt Manor, NY 10567
Telephone: (914) 736-0428
Fax: (914) 736-0428
E-mail: jsewsall@optonline.net
Window treatment designer, installer, workroom
Juanita Strassfield

One Day Decorating
9900 Peach St.
Waterford, PA 16441
Telephone: (814) 796-6597
Website: www.onedaydecorating.com
*Interior redesign specialist who uses existing furnish-
ings to give your home a fresh new look*

One Lake Design
Round Rock, TX 78664-9415
Telephone: (512) 255-9110
Fax: (512) 238-6463
Website: www.onelakedesign.com
Licensed interior design firm with 20 years experience

Paolina's Custom Draperies
6620 Cobb Dr.
Sterling Hts., MI 48312
Telephone: (800) 974-3433, (586) 977-9304
Fax: (586) 977-0269
Website: www.paolinasdraperies.com
E-mail: info@paolinasdraperies.com
*Custom window treatments, bedding and other home
accessories*

Personal Statements
7 Barnard Rd.
Marlboro, MA 01752-1543
Telephone: (508) 481-6324
Fax: (508) 481-1686
E-mail: carsackler@aol.com
Window treatment designer, workroom
Carol Sackler

Phil Hugh Smith
108 South Main St.
Cohasset, MA 02025
Telephone: (781) 383-0549
E-mail: philiphughsmith@verizon.net

Prosperity Interiors, Inc.
Studio: 272 Newtown Ave.
Norwalk, CT 06851
Studio Telephone: (203) 847-7681
Mailing Address: 18 Sturges Commons
Westport, CT 06880
Office Telephone: (203) 255-2734
Website: www.prosperityinteriors.com
E-mail: Lamydesign@aol.com
Susan Lamy

Royal Window & Interior Fashions
1105 E 34th St.
Brooklyn, NY 11210
Telephone: (718) 252-1166
Fax: (718) 252-3671
E-mail: royalwindow-interior@verizon.net
*Comprehensive window treatments, bedding, throw
pillows, table linens/runners and decorative machine
embroidery*
Althea E. Russell-Anglin/Everett Russell

Ruffell & Brown Interiors
2745 Bridge St.
Victoria, BC
Telephone: (250) 384-1230
Fax: (250) 384-0204
Website: www.ruffell-brown.com
E-mail: sales@ruffell-brown.com
*Comprehensive interior design center: custom window
treatments, drapery hardware, upholstery, interior
shutters, closet organizers, fine wall coverings and tap-
estries, installation and repairs, custom furniture, bed-
ding, motorization, more*

Sally's Interiors
985 Marina Dr.
Napa, CA 94559
Telephone: (707) 224-6972
Fax: (707) 224-6972
E-mail: Sal4phil@aol.com
*ASID design firm—creating beautiful interiors at an
affordable price*

Scot Robbins & Co.
4028 Port Victoria Ct.
Hermitage, TN 37076-3123
Telephone: (615) 391-5772
Website: www.scotrobbins.com
J. Scot Robbins

Sew Beautiful
509 Red Bluff Ct.
Millersville, MD 21108
Telephone: (410) 987-5084
Fax: (410) 987-5086
E-mail: sewbeautiful@cablespeed.com
*Design and fabrication of custom window treatments
and soft furnishings*
Margaret Blunt

Shelby Upholstering & Interior
3136 W 16th St.
Indianapolis, IN 46222
Telephone: (317) 631-8911, (800) 331-7697
Fax: (317) 631-9999
Website: www.shelbyupholstering.com
E-mail: sales@shelbyupholstering.com
*Custom window treatments, complete interiors:
everything for your business, church or home*

Signature Draperies & Design
1510 Topar Ave.
Los Altos, CA 94024
Telephone: (650) 949-5100
E-mail: sandypowell@mindspring.com
*Custom draperies, roman shades, blinds, top-treatments
and upholstery; member ASID, WFCP*
Sandy Powell, CWTC CWTC

Simply Elegant Solutions
4897 Dovecote Trail
Suwanee, GA 30024-4198
Telephone: (678) 482-2052
Fax: (678) 482-7689
E-mail: cindyvin@bellsouth.net
*Completely custom solutions for every decorating
dilemma*
Cindy Vincent

Stafford Decors
315 Garrisonville Rd.
Stafford, VA 22554
Telephone: (540) 659-7808
Fax: (540) 659-0908
E-mail: decorslda@aol.com
Custom window treatments and decorating retail store
Heather Goldberg

Sumptuous Living
43646 Cypress Village Dr.
Ashburn, VA 20147
Serving Northern Virginia, Loudoun
County in particular
Telephone: (703) 880-4969
Fax: (703) 880-4974
E-mail: macarena@sumptuousliving.com
Interior decorating and custom draperies
Macarena Janninck

Susan Gill Workroom
208 W 30 St., Ste. 1106
New York, NY 10001
Telephone: (212) 629-6127
Fax: (262) 967-9860
E-mail: susangill@earthlink.net
Window treatment designer, workroom
Susan Gill

Susan Schurz
Telephone: (804) 690-9175
E-mail: Tavernhill@aol.com
To the trade drapery workroom
Tavern Hill

Suzanne Marie's Interiors
2329 Crestmont Cir. S
PO Box 4775
Salem, OR 97302
Telephone: (503) 364-4237
Fax: (503) 391-2362

SWAG Designs
Telephone: (415) 887-9024
Fax: (415) 887-9025
Website: www.swagdesigns.com
E-mail: lynnamon@swagdesigns.com
*Custom design service, including window treatments.
By appointment*
Lynn Amon

Tony Caso Designs
275 Omaha St.
Palm Harbor, FL 34683
Telephone: (727) 786-7868
Fax: (727) 786-7548
Website: www.tcdesigns.home.att.net
E-Mail: tcdesigns@worldnet.att.net
Drapery and upholstery workroom, custom cabinetry

Treatments For Your Panes
727 Wood Hill Dr.
Macedon, NY 14502
Telephone: (315) 986-3106
Fax: (315) 986-3106
E-mail: dwilli12@rochester.rr.com
Window treatment designer, installer, workroom
Deborah Williamson
Treating Spaces
32 Angelica Dr.
Framingham, MA 01701
Telephone: (508) 405-1233
E-mail: treatingsspaces@ren.com
Lee Ann Price, CWTC

The Ultimate Install
23724 NE 65th Pl.
Redmond, WA 98053
Telephone: (866) 936-3731
Fax: (425) 836-3731
E-mail: theultimateinstall@comcast.net
Window treatment design and installation
Cherie Hollenbeck

Unique Expressions
1608 E Chippewa River Rd.
Midland, MI 48640
Telephone: (877) 516-4677, (989) 832-0250
Fax: (989) 636-7342
E-mail: uniqshasta@charter.net
Shasta personally visits customers in the state of Michigan to provide current information and new products offered by her vendors. Please call to make an appointment if you are interested.
Shasta Breitkopf

Valerie Sutherland Window Fashions
316 A St.
Encinitas, CA 92024
Telephone: (760) 635-7939
Valerie Sutherland

Vera Orgera Interior Design
2341 Mitchell Rd.
Marietta, GA 30062
Telephone: (404) 663-3229
Fax: (770) 973-9090
E-mail: vera@vointeriordesign.com
Full service interior design
Vera Orgera

Wallflowers
1340 Rosedale Ln.
Hoffman Estates, IL 60195
707 Skokie Blvd., Ste. 600
Northbrook, IL 60062
1450 Mitchell Blvd.
Design Center

Schaumburg, IL 60193
Telephone: (847) 433 2890
E-mail: tazagore@aol.com
A full-service interior design studio with a focus on residential interior design offering a complete range of services

Well Dressed Windows, Inc.
6450 Windy Willow Dr.
Solon, OH 44139
Telephone: (440) 498-9119
Fax: (440) 248-9285
Website: www.dressedwindows.com
E-mail: info@dressedwindows.com
High quality window treatments and great service, at an affordable price
Eileen Zimmerman

Window Accents, Inc.
836 Francisco Blvd. W
San Rafael, CA 94901
Telephone: (415) 459-7838
Fax: (415) 457-6479
E-mail: jhenson@windowaccents.com
John Henson

Windows by Betty
7624 Chancellor Way
Springfield, VA 22153
Telephone: (703) 455-2231
Fax: (703) 455-2231
E-mail: BeachFerg@aol.com
Window treatment designer, workroom
Betty Ferguson

Windows by Design
21 Longview Dr.
Elkton, MD 21921
Telephone: (410) 398-5922
E-mail: athomemichelle@comcast.net
Window treatment design and fabrication
Michelle Ness, CWP

Workroom
1906 W Belmont Ave.
Chicago, IL 60657
Telephone: (773) 472-2140
Website: www.workroominc.com
Full range of window treatments, art design products, interiors
Joel Klaff and John Diekmann

Yardstick Drapes
110564 Da Anza Blvd.
Cupertino, CA 95014
Telephone: (800) 480-0788, (408) 366-1424
Fax: (408) 265-5942
Website: www.yardstickdrapes.com
E-mail: jack@yardstickdrapes.com
Custom window coverings, reupholstery, redecorating and interior design services